SILVER

for pleasure and investment

SILVER

for pleasure and investment

GEOFFREY WILLS

JOHN GIFFORD · LONDON

First published 1969 by
John Gifford Ltd.,
125 Charing Cross Road,
London WC2

SBN 70710271 5

Text and plates printed in Great Britain
by Compton Printing Ltd.
London and Aylesbury

Acknowledgements

The author is grateful to the County Museum, Truro, Cornwall, for permission to photograph the articles in Plates 2, 5, 7, and 11, to Christie's, London, for Plate 1, and to the undermentioned for the supply of photographs:

The Worshipful Company of Goldsmiths, London: figs. 1, 3.

Bearnes, Torquay, Devon: figs. 12, 20, 58, 61, 85.

Christie's, London: figs. 5, 6, 8, 10, 11, 13, 17, 18, 19, 22, 24, 25, 30, 32, 33, 34, 35, 39, 47, 49, 50, 52, 54, 57, 62, 65, 66, 70, 77a,78, 82, 86, 89, 92, 93, 96, 97, 99, 100.

Graves, Son & Pilcher, Hove, Sussex: figs. 4, 56.

King & Chasemore, Pulborough, Sussex: figs. 29, 55, 63, 79.

Parke-Bernet Galleries, Inc., New York: figs. 7, 40, 91, 94.

Phillips, Son & Neale, London: figs. 41, 42.

Sotheby's, London: figs. 16, 28, 36, 37, 38, 46, 51, 53, 59, 71, 72, 74, 76, 95.

Henry Spencer & Sons, Retford, Nottinghamshire: figs. 31, 64, 77.

Also Denise Poole Ltd., Alford, Lincs.

Author's Note

While the word 'investment' appears in the sub-title and may lead a reader to expect some kind of list of prices, none has been provided. Such guides are of little or no use through being out-dated as soon as they are written. They can refer only to a particular item on a particular occasion, whether in an auction-room or a shop, and generalisations are not helpful in connexion with antiques. Thus, the only worthwhile course for a potential buyer is to go to a reputable dealer and remember the epigram of Benvenuto Cellini, the sixteenth century Florentine artist, silver-smith and sculptor. His words, which incidentally form the motto of the British Antique Dealers' Association, were: *Ars non habet inimicum nisi ignorantiam*: *Art has no enemy except ignorance*. It is to be hoped that this book will contribute to the reader's knowledge and enjoyment, and enable him to invest with confidence.

Geoffrey Wills.

CONTENTS

List of Colour Plates

List of Black & White Photographs

List of Black & White Photographs

List of Black & White Photographs

List of Black & White Photographs

Introduction

Old English silver has in its favour a number of qualities that have for a long time ensured it a high place among collectors' favourite subjects. Not least, when considerations of finance are important, is the fact that the metal itself has a commercial value throughout the world.

Silver, is esteemed not only on account of its beauty when polished, but because it is adaptable to such a diversity of forms. Anyone beginning to study the subject may be surprised to find that the metal has been made into such a very wide range of articles. They vary not only in shape but also in decoration, and in the following pages the reader will find descriptions and illustrations of both the rare and the less rare.

The principal concern of the book is with the domestic wares produced during the eighteenth century, but those made before and after receive a mention where appropriate. While Georgian silver is scarcer than that of later date, it is by no means as difficult to find as that of the preceding centuries and it remains the most favoured by the majority of people. During the hundred years many styles came and went, and among them there must be at least one to suit every taste. Nineteenth century productions remain more limited in appeal, although in due course they will come to be accepted more widely.

1. Assaying

Silver is found in the earth in conjunction with other metals, amalgamated with mercury and, occasionally, in almost pure form. Supplies in the eighteenth century came principally from South America, where the Potosi mines in Bolivia and the many workings on the slopes of the Andes, in Peru, produced enormous quantities. The ore was treated on the spot, and where coal or timber were lacking for roasting it, recourse was had to dried llama dung and a suitable local fungus. Further to the north, in Mexico, were equally important and vast deposits of silver, and the whole had had the eager attention of European adventurers since the sixteenth century when the Spaniards had first colonised the continent.

The ingots were brought across the Atlantic in galleons, which were the prey of those who sought a quick fortune. A famous and successful instance occurred in June, 1743, while the English were at war with Spain. The 'Centurion', commanded by the future Admiral Lord Anson, captured the fully-laden 'Nuestra Senora de Covadonga', and reached London in triumph two years later. It was reported that the booty amounted to

2,600,000 Pieces of Eight, 150,000 Ounces of Plate, 10 Bars of Gold, and a large Quantity of Gold and Silver Dust; in the whole to the Amount of 1,250,000 l. Sterling.

On 4th July, a Wednesday, the same journal noted:

Passed thro' St. James's-street, the Strand, Cheapside, &c., in their Way to the Tower, 32 Waggons from Portsmouth, with the Treasure

Plate 1   2
Urn ornamented with fluting and with embossed and chased swags of flowers, the base cast. Apparently no maker's mark, 1770. Height 24½ inches. Weight 98 oz. 3 dwt. (scratched weight).

brought home by Admiral Anson; they were guarded by the Ship's Crew (which consisted of many Nations) and preceded by the Officers, with Swords drawn, Musick playing and Colours flying, particularly that of the Acapulca Prize.

The softness of pure or *fine* silver is one of its characteristics, and anything made from it would withstand very little handling. It is only excelled by gold as a malleable and ductile metal, and a piece of it weighing a gramme can be drawn out into a wire no less than 180 metres in length. It can be appreciated, therefore, that articles made from it would prove impracticably short-lived in use.

To give it strength, and yet preserve its distinctive and agreeable appearance, it has been invariably alloyed with another metal: copper. The amount of the latter employed is of great concern, because it is of a very low monetary value in comparison with the silver. Unscrupulous workers from time immemorial seized the opportunity to secretly increase the proportion of the base metal and thus raise their own profit.

Until the sixteenth century the ancient 'Tower' pound, divided into marks, shillings and pence, was employed for weighing silver. It was replaced by the 'Troy' pound, which is divisible as follows:

Pounds	Ounces	Pennyweights	Grains
1	12	240	5,760
	1	20	480
		1	24

The ounce is equivalent to 31·1 grammes.

Troy weight has been used continuously since it was introduced from Troyes, in eastern France, during the reign of Henry VIII. It may be noted that two customs are observed in using it: the pennyweight is written *dwt*, and the weight of the metal is never expressed in pounds or *lbs*. However heavy a piece may be, its weight is given in ounces and pennyweights (*oz.* and *dwt.*).

For many centuries laws have been passed making it an offence to vary the quantity of copper over and above the legal amount. In the measured words of an authority writing in 1852:

> No fraud could be practised so successfully, either as to escaping detection, or as to reaping large pecuniary profits, as the selling adulterated gold and silver plate, did not the law lend its especial aids to the purchasers of these wares.

The importance of protecting the buyer becomes plain when it is realised that almost an equal weight of alloy can be added to the silver before its presence becomes clearly visible.

Plate 2   3

Caddy spoon with cast bowl. By William Pugh, Birmingham, 1807. Length 2½ inches.—Caddy spoon in the form of a hand. Maker's mark I S, *circa* 1820.—Fish slice with pierced and engraved blade. By John Younge & Co., Sheffield, 1783; handle, by William Sutton. Length 12⅝ inches.—Sifter spoon. By Joseph Taylor, Birmingham, 1802. Length 2½ inches.

In A.D. 1300 the standard alloy of silver and copper for both coinage and vessels was laid down by statute. It was, and is, known as Sterling standard and was once thought to have gained its name from some connexion with the Scottish town of Stirling. Writing of it in his *Britannia*, William Camden, who lived between 1551 and 1623, noted:

But they are much mistaken, that think our good and lawful money of England, commonly called Sterling-money, takes its name from hence: for that denomination came from the Germans, termed Easterlings by the English, from their living Eastward, who were first called in by K. John of England, to reduce the Silver to its due fineness: and such money in antient writings is always termed Easterling.

Sterling silver is composed of 11 oz. 2 dwt. of pure or *fine* metal with 18 dwt, of copper, making a pound Troy. These proportions result in an alloy which is not too difficult to work and can be formed into durable articles of numerous kinds. During most of the past centuries the coinage has been of Sterling standard, although from time to time, and in the present century, varying quantities of copper and other metals have been added while the silver content has been correspondingly reduced.

During the Civil War and under the rule of Cromwell very large quantities of silverware were melted down to mint currency for paying the troops on each side, and for issue by the Treasury for use in daily commerce. When the monarchy was restored in 1660 there remained only a small fraction of the plate that had existed when Charles I had been on the throne. The reign of Charles II saw the growth of a fashion for luxury and ostentation in complete contrast to the years of austerity preceding it, and there was a big demand for silver. To satisfy it, the silversmiths took current coinage, melted it and re-made it into useful or decorative articles.

To prevent this abuse, which was leading to disastrous results economically, the standard of Sterling silver for vessels was raised while that for the coinage remained unaltered. Instead of comprising 11 oz. 2 dwt. of fine silver and 18 dwt. of alloy to the Troy pound, it was raised to 11 oz. 10 dwt. of fine silver and 10 dwt. of alloy. The difference of 8 dwt. was sufficient to prevent the mis-use of silver coins, and at the same time citizens were invited to sell their plate of the old Sterling standard to the Mint at the price of 5s. 4d. an ounce.

The eye alone cannot be relied upon to detect the fraudulent adulteration of silver, and it must be tested by a more reliable method. At first, this was done by means of the touchstone: a fine-grained hard black stone, of which, incidentally, it is said that good imitations were made in Wedgwood's basaltes: a hard black pottery. The touchstone was rubbed on the article being tested, and then a comparison was made between the mark on the stone and the mark made on it by known pure silver. Alternatively, accord-

4

ing to a writer in 1667, 'wet all the touched places [on the stone] with your tongue, and it will show itself in its own countenance.'

A touchstone can give little more than a rough indication to its user, and is more successful in determining the purity of gold than that of silver. For true accuracy it is necessary to have recourse to assaying and obtain a result that is beyond doubt. Although the procedure is somewhat complicated it has remained in continual use since it was introduced more than six centuries ago.

Briefly, the assayer takes the tiny portion of metal to be tested, weighs it carefully and wraps it in a thin piece of lead. This is put in a crucible made of bone-ash, animal bones burned to a white powder, which is placed in a furnace. The bone-ash container, known as a *cupel*, has the property of absorbing base metals, and on being raised to melting heat these vanish to leave only the fine silver. When it is cool the pellet of silver is weighed, and the resultant figure compared with the weight before assay. The proportion of alloy formerly present can be easily calculated, and if of Sterling standard or higher the appropriate marks are stamped on the article from which the sample was taken.

Assaying was, and still is, carried out by the London and provincial Goldsmiths Companies. The sequence of testing and marking begins when a silversmith becomes a member and enters his name and mark with one of the Companies; usually the one nearest to his workshop. The mark he has chosen for himself is cut on a steel punch so that it can be stamped on his work, and its maker can thereby be identified.

After he has almost completed an article and it requires little more than finishing, the silversmith takes it to the assay office where his name is entered. Between 1784 and 1890, when duty was payable, he also wrote details of his work on a slip of paper and paid the sum due. The wardens and assayer of the Company examine the article, check that it bears the maker's mark and whether it has been constructed with overmuch solder; the latter affecting the final weight and equalling an overall lowering of the silver Standard.

If these conditions have not been fulfilled the work is rejected, but if all is well the next step is taken. A small amount of metal is scraped from the article and given to the assayer. The scraping must weigh no more than four grains in each twelve ounces of the piece, and is normally taken from the underside or wherever it will cause the least disfigurement. Old silver articles sometimes retain the mark where the original assay scraping, or a subsequent one, was taken, but usually the maker polished out the disturbed surface.

Provided the assay shows that the silver content of the sample is correct, the piece is then given the appropriate marks confirming the fact. If not,

5

two further assays are made, and then if the article fails to pass the tests it is cut through and the remains returned to the maker, but this is an exceptional occurrence. Fully marked, the article is taken back to the work shop for finishing and is then ready for sale. In practice, the sequence was not always strictly followed, and pieces are known which lack full or correct sets of marks (see page 7 and Plate 5).

Some idea of the quantity of silverware manufactured towards the end of the eighteenth century is to be gained from figures given before a committee of the House of Commons. They covered the years 1766 to 1772:

	oz.	dwt.
1766	1,884,651	3
1767	2,032,070	11
1768	1,918,182	10
1769	1,960,224	19
1770	1,965,348	16
1771	1,997,228	17
1772	2,092,824	15

In comparison, the same committee learned of the weight of silver 'broken and defaced' for being below standard. For the same period of seven years it totalled 168,262 oz. 16 dwt. which is roughly 12½ per cent compared with the amount, noted above, of Sterling quality.

There have always been penalties, varying in their severity from time to time, payable by those breaking the various laws concerned with the making and selling of silverware. At one period death was the reward of anyone who forged the sovereign's head or duty mark or who transposed marks from one piece to another, and the forging of marks other than the duty mark resulted in transportation for fourteen years. Similarly assayers could be fined £200, no small sum 150 years ago, if they marked any article except in the presence of two wardens, or mark it before assayed and found standard, or discover any pattern, design or invention of any ware brought to be assayed, or suffer it to be viewed by any person not necessarily employed in the office. In addition to a heavy fine, the guilty assayer would suffer dismissal from his job and be prohibited from filling a similar position again.

In spite of these and other deterrents, a variety of frauds have been practised at different periods. The most common of them take the form of what are termed 'duty dodgers': articles made and sold without payment of duty. While the duty of 1784–1890 required proof in the form of a mark that it had been paid, an earlier tax did not. In 1719 sixpence per ounce was levied on all assayed ware, it was collected by the Excise Department of the Government but no particulars have been published stating exactly how this was carried out. It was eventually found unsatisfactory and was abandoned in 1757.

The duty was 'dodged' by two methods. The first was by the simple expedient of transposing the marked portion of a piece of low value that had been assayed in the normal manner. Such actions are not easy to detect, and are usually only brought to light when there is an obvious difference between the style of a piece and the date of its marking, or when it is known that a maker had died before a particular form of article came into use. An important ewer in the Victoria and Albert Museum bears the transposed mark of Paul de Lamerie and the date-letter for 1736.

The second form of 'duty-dodging' came about through an assumption that articles made to order from old and assayed silver were exempt from further testing. Not being submitted for examination meant that they paid no tax. It was a common practice for what were considered old-fashioned pieces to be taken to a silversmith who allowed the weight of metal against the purchase of something new.

Instances of such transactions occur in the account-book kept by John Hervey, first Earl of Bristol, and although they pre-date the duty, they and similar records show that exchanges of this kind were not uncommon. One of Hervey's entries reads:

November 7th, 1696: Paid Mr Edw: Waldegrave, a goldsmith in Russel street, for 11 dishes, 1 dozen of plates, a coffee pott, & a porridg laddle, weighing 802 ounces, at 5s. 3¼d. per ounce, & for ye graving, £211. 7s. £7. 3s. in mony, ye rest in old plate of my dear fathers.

The proportion of surviving silverware which bears no more than a maker's mark on it suggests that the custom was not uncommon. Thus, pieces of the type were not necessarily of poor metal, and do not differ basically from fully-marked specimens. The latter realise the higher prices when sold and, strictly speaking, unmarked, partly-marked or deceptively-marked specimens remain liable to be seized by the Goldsmiths' Company. If taken and found to be below Sterling standard they would be broken, and if they successfully pass the assay any old marks are defaced and replaced by correct modern ones.

The marks already discussed were all stamped with steel punches, but much old silver bears engraved numerals that are usually on the underside of an article where they will not normally be noticed. They refer to the weight of the piece and are given in ounces and pennyweights: thus, 12/12 for 12 oz. 12 dwt. Generations of industrious butlers, housekeepers and housewives have in most cases rubbed away some of the silver, and a comparison between what is termed the 'scratched weight' and that at the present time will reveal how much has vanished in the intervening period.

Such a disparity can total quite a few pennyweights if alterations have been made to an article; for instance if an old crest, or a monogram, has been erased.

A knowledge of the weight of a piece can be a useful clue to its quality; a silversmith would not stint himself in the use of metal for an important order. Whereas for everyday articles each ounce was watched in order to keep the selling-price as low as possible. The majority of old silver of a definite period, say sauceboats made in and around the year 1760, will be found to weigh within a matter of pennyweights of each other, but the few of superior quality will be noticeably heavier.

At one time, until about the thirties of this century, it was commonplace for silverware to be sold by auction at so much an ounce. The inexperienced salegoer would have to be quick at mental arithmetic if he ventured to bid, and there are a number of stories current about those who imagined they had bought bargains. One can picture an innocent noticing a salver going for 50/s., hiding his glee while stealthily bidding to 55/s., and hearing the hammer fall. The luckless buyer would then find he had become the owner of something weighing 100 oz. or so, and costing him in the region of £275.

Nowadays, pieces are sold at so much per lot; the latter comprising several small items or a single one worth £10 or more. Typical catalogue entries would read as follows:

65 Three pairs of Georgian Sugar Tongs in various designs; three other pairs, one formed as a wishbone; two Sugar Sifters; a crested Fish Slice with pierced blades and sprung upper arm, an odd Teaspoon, Georgian and later dates, 15 oz. 1 dwt.; and four plated Sauce Ladles with spirally fluted stems.

195 A George II shaped circular Salver on three hoof supports, 6¼ in. diameter, by Robert Abercromby, 1738, 7 oz. 11 dwt.

The exact silver content of some pieces cannot be weighed without difficulty. They include certain types of candlestick, which were given a heavy internal packing of cast-iron or lead to make them stable. Equally, teapots, coffee pots and jugs with wood or ivory handles and knobs would have to have these parts dismantled before their actual silver content could be gauged. In such instances, descriptions which include the weight usually record it with the terms 'gross weight' or 'all in', which mean that the article has been weighed as it stands and the figures include wood, ivory and any other material forming a part of it.

8

2. Hall-marks

The study of English silver is made comparatively easy by the system of hallmarking, by which almost every specimen is required by law to be stamped as a warranty of its genuineness. It enables most old silver to be dated closely, its maker to be named and the buyer to be protected against fraud. It is the last of these considerations which instigated the introduction of the practice.

The workers in gold and silver, collectively termed goldsmiths whichever metal they used, framed their own rules from very early times. This was not only to protect the public from fraud, but to forestall outside interference with their conduct. Once they had organised themselves satisfactorily and were able to guarantee their own integrity, the members were recognised by King, Parliament and public. To these early craftsmen is due the esteem enjoyed by their numerous successors; an esteem that has remained unimpaired over the intervening centuries down to the present day.

The first recorded evidence of the existence of a Goldsmiths' Company in England dates back to the year 1180. Then, a group of them was fined for having been inaugurated without first obtaining permission from the reigning monarch, Henry II. Successive statutes related to the quality of silver and gold used, and prohibited the importation of foreign coins that were mostly of poor metal. In 1300 an Act of Edward I provided that no ware should be offered for sale until it had been tested by the 'Gardiens of the Craft', and bore a mark on it in the shape of a leopard's head. It was the

9

forerunner of many such laws, which together resulted in the establishment of the system of hallmarking.

The London guild of goldsmiths was incorporated in a correct manner in 1327, and acquired the resounding title of 'The Wardens and Commonalty of the Mystery of the Goldsmiths of the City of London.' Its headquarters are on land owned by the guild since about 1323, and the present Goldsmiths' Hall dates from 1835. Designed by Philip Hardwick, who built Euston railway-station and the lamented archway that once stood before it, it replaces a building erected by Sir Christopher Wren following the Great Fire.

The leopard's head was designated the 'King's Mark', and was an assurance to purchasers that pieces bearing it were of the required standard. The head was actually that of a lion, but was misnamed owing to confusion in translating a word written in the old French language. The head was used occasionally in the provinces, but duly became recognised as the mark of the London assay-office. A figure of a lion *passant* (walking) was adopted as the sign for Sterling silver.

The use of the leopard's head was intended to guarantee the metal, but was apparently insufficient to prevent fraud. Malpractices continued, and in order to bring the offenders to justice it was enacted that each maker should put a personal stamp on his wares. This was made law in 1363, and fifteen years later a further Act stated that:

... because gold and silver, which is wrought by goldsmiths in England, is oftentimes less fine than it ought to be, because the goldsmiths are their own judges, be it ordained that henceforth every goldsmith put his own mark upon his work.

It was decreed also that anyone not properly marking his goods or using silver of a lower standard than that required 'shall pay to the party complaining double the value of the vessel, and be put in prison, and pay a fine according to the extent of the trespass.'

From the frequency with which such laws were passed it can be deduced that there continued to be considerable evasion, and Parliament devoted much time to the subject. A principal concern was that the silver and gold coinage should not be debased. It was a simple matter to take coins and melt them along with some base metal to produce a profitable article. Had this been allowed to take place on a large scale the currency of the realm would soon have vanished.

To the same end, there were strict regulations about the import and export of gold and silver. An Act of 1381 made the consequences quite clear:

For the great mischief which the realm suffereth and long hath done, for that gold and silver as well in money as in plate and jewels as other-

10

wise by exchanges made in divers manners is carried out in the realm so that in effect there is none left, which thing, if it should be longer suffered, would shortly be the destruction of the same realm, which God forbid.

The early goldsmiths used pictorial signs for their shops and workshops, and models of them or paintings on boards were hung outside the premises. Similar signs were adopted for personal marks on their handiwork, and such things as a fish, a bird's head and a key are among the many that have been recorded. Unfortunately, none can now be allied to the name of a particular maker.

Then, in 1478 a third mark was added. It took the form of a letter of the alphabet, was known at first as the 'Warden's Mark', and from it the warden of the Company responsible for testing an article could be readily identified. It was changed annually, as were the responsible officers, and thus it had a secondary meaning in indicating the date of the assay. As this normally took place very soon after manufacture (or prior to the final finishing) it is usual to refer to the letter mark as denoting the year when the piece was actually made.

The alphabet employed by the Goldsmiths' Company was one of twenty letters, and lacked J, U or V, W, X, Y and Z. When the end of each short series had been reached a fresh one of a different form was commenced. Thus, the Gothic u of 1578 was followed by a Roman capital A, and there were also changes from time to time in the outer shaping of the stamp. Theoretically it should always be possible to distinguish one set of markings from another, but in practice it has been found that ambiguities are occasionally met with.

As the London wardens were, and still are, elected yearly in May each date-letter covers half of two succeeding years: say, from May 1758 to May 1759, and the corresponding date-letter, a Gothic capital ℭ thus stands for either of those years. To be precise in the matter, pieces bearing it should be described as having been made in 1758/9, but it is usually sufficient to quote only the earlier of the dates.

The higher standard silver introduced at the end of the seventeenth century (see page 4) was distinctively stamped with a figure of Britannia. At the same time, the leopard's head was withdrawn from use and replaced by a lion's head *erased*: namely, turned to one side and with the neck ending in three tabs, looking as if it had been torn from the body of the animal.

When introducing the new Britannia Standard, which came into force on 27th March 1697, the authorities took the opportunity to make fresh rules concerning makers' marks. Thenceforward they were to bear the first two letters of the surname, and this endured until 1st June 1720. In the

11

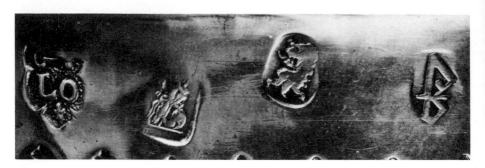

Fig. 1
London hallmark, Britannia standard, 1705. (Left to right): maker's mark of Nathaniel Lock, figure of Britannia, lion's head erased, and date letter.

latter year the initials of Christian name and surname were ordered to be used on Sterling silver, which is the practice today, but for Britannia standard metal the old form was continued. Having two styles of marking was found to cause confusion, and in 1739 all makers were ordered to have completely different stamps from those employed before and all of them should show their initials. Thus, in 1712 Paul de Lamerie entered at Goldsmiths' Hall a mark with a crown above a star and the letters LA over a fleur-de-lys. To comply with the new regulation he changed it in 1739 to the script letters $\mathcal{P}\mathcal{L}$ with a crown above and a star or dot below, replacing the stamp with Roman letters he had entered in 1724.

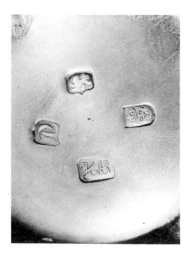

Fig. 2
London hallmark, 1774. (Clockwise from top): lion *passant*, crowned leopard's head, maker's mark of Hester Bateman, and date letter.

12

By 1719 the country had achieved a more settled state, and the Britannia standard ceased to be compulsory. It could still be used if desired, and continues to be employed occasionally at the present time. The former Sterling standard was restored, and the majority of plate made from then onwards complied with its requirements. For the latter, the lion *passant* was again used, but Britannia standard at any date is signified by the familiar seated female holding an oval shield and a trident. It is said that the original model for her was Frances Stuart, Duchess of Richmond and Lennox, mistress of Charles II.

The writer of a book on silversmithing published in 1677 stated that there was then at the assay office a list of the names of all craftsmen. Against each name was an impression of the man's personal mark, so the wardens might ensure 'that the marks be plain and of a fit size, and not one like another.' The Company could in this way make certain that the marks were identifiable beyond doubt.

The list had survived the Great Fire, which took place in 1666, but perished at some time after 1677. It has been suggested that it was destroyed deliberately, and a probable reason would be that it had become out of date. There remain at present a copper plate struck with the marks of makers working in 1675, and books of names and marks from 1697 onwards. The books were commenced on April 15th of the year, following introduction of the Britannia standard. Each entry gives the silversmith's name followed by his mark, and they form the basis of our knowledge of old silver and its makers. Apart from the lack of some pages, which have been torn out, and the absence of a few of the complete volumes, the series of books is at Goldsmiths' Hall, London, and is kept up to date.

Fig. 3
London hallmark, 1810. (Left to right):
maker's mark of Paul Storr, lion *passant*,
crowned leopard's head, date letter, and
head of George III denoting duty had
been paid. These marks and those in the
preceding illustrations were not always
stamped in the same order.

13

One further, important, mark has now to be noted: the Duty mark. From 1st December 1784, Parliament re-imposed the duty of 6d. an ounce which had ceased to be levied in 1758. It was calculated on five-sixths of the weight of each article with the odd sixth allowed for waste in finishing. Over the years the duty was increased and by 1815 it had trebled, but no further rises took place after that date.

When the silversmith took or sent his work to be assayed he was required to pay the duty at the same time, and in proof of payment his work was stamped with the head of the reigning sovereign. The heads of the Kings concerned, George III, George IV and William IV are all depicted facing to the right, but Queen Victoria is to the left. There was one exception, when George III was for a short period shown looking to the left, and the stamp used resulted in his head appearing *incuse*: sunken instead of raised. The incuse punch was in use only between 1st December 1784 and 29th May 1785, so examples showing it are not common.

Finally, in 1790, to clear up existing confusion, certain articles were exempted by Parliament from payment of duty. They did not require to be assayed and therefore need only bear the maker's mark or could go completely unmarked. The Act specified exemption for 'Silver Wares not weighing 5 dwt. of Silver each', *except*:

Mounts for bottles in cruet-frames.
Buttons and certain types of studs.
Bottle tickets (now better known as Wine-labels)
Patch boxes.
Salt spoons, ladles and shovels.
Tea strainers and caddy-spoons.
'Pieces to garnish Cabinets or Knife Cases, or Tea Chests, or Bridles, or Stands, or Frames.'

Thus, the foregoing pieces, and a few others of lesser interest, should have been submitted for assay, and marked after payment of duty on them. They are found, however, sometimes with only a maker's mark and the lion *passant*.

On 1st May 1890 the duty was no longer payable, and the sovereign's head ceased to be used as a mark. Thus, any piece of silver bearing one of the heads on it can be dated between 1784 and 1890. These are hardly narrow limits, but sometimes are a useful quick guide. Again, exceptions exist, and in 1953 souvenirs to celebrate the coronation of Queen Elizabeth II were given marks which included the head of the Queen, while in 1933–35 a stamp was used with the heads of George V and Queen Mary. Some of these pieces were made of Britannia standard silver, and accordingly bore the Britannia mark and the lion's head *erased*.

14

The foregoing remarks apply to silverware assayed at Goldsmiths' Hall, in the City of London. From time to time testing and hallmarking were carried out at a number of provincial towns and cities. This was obviously desirable wherever there were sufficient craftsmen working to justify it, as it was both time-consuming and expensive to send everything to London for the purpose.

As early as 1410 the authorities at York had been assaying and marking locally-made work, and in 1423 it was enacted that this might be done also at Newcastle-upon-Tyne, Lincoln, Norwich, Bristol, Salisbury and Coventry. However, some of these towns were not eager to avail themselves of the privilege, and others appointed themselves as additional assaying centres. There has been research into what mark or marks was used by each of them, but the picture remains far from clear. The use of date-letters outside London was slow to be accepted, and did not begin at York until 1559 or at Norwich until 1565. In 1700 Goldsmiths' Companies were incorporated and assaying authorised at York, Exeter, Bristol, Chester and Norwich, and in the following year Newcastle-upon-Tyne was added to the list. Finally, in 1773 both Birmingham and Sheffield obtained Parliamentary permission to establish assay-offices.

The procedure at each of the provincial centres was modelled on that in London, and the marks employed were of the same kind. Each used the lion *passant* to denote Sterling standard, but although date-letters were used in the same manner they did not correspond each year with those of the capital. Likewise, the day on which new alphabets were introduced annually varied from place to place. Most important, the London leopard's head was not employed, but was replaced by a distinctive mark for each office.

The marks used by the provincial assay-offices were as follows:

York: a cross on which are five lions *passant*. The office was not in operation between 1713 and 1770 and closed finally in 1856.

Exeter: a castle with three towers (see Newcastle). Closed in 1882.

Bristol: a ship sailing from behind a castle. Examples of its use are very rare.

Chester: a shield with three half-lions used until 1779, when a new mark with three wheatsheaves and a sword was adopted.

Norwich: a castle above a lion was used as the town-mark, and a crowned Tudor rose to denote Sterling silver. Examples are very rare.

Newcastle-upon-Tyne: three separate towers, two above and one below and not joined together as at Exeter. The office closed in 1883.

Birmingham: an anchor.

Sheffield: a crown. Sometimes stamped separately, and sometimes combined with the date-letter.

15

Similar conditions existed north of the Border, in Scotland, and the Edinburgh goldsmiths were active from an early date. Records are preserved dating back to 1525, and these give the names of the various officials concerned in administering the craft. As in England, Statutes were passed to regulate the purity of the metal and prescribing punishments for infringements of the law. The City used the triple-towered castle from its coat of arms as a mark, and added to it were those of the maker and the deacon of the company at the time. This endured until 1681, when date-letters were commenced in place of the last-named stamp.

At Glasgow the town mark comprised a combination of a tree, a salmon and a bell, with or without a capital letter G. As at Edinburgh, date-letters were in use from 1681. Aberdeen, Greenock, and a few other towns also assayed the work of their citizens, and each used a distinctive mark or marks.

In Ireland, silversmiths are known to have been working before the Norman Conquest, and the names of some of them are given in documents dating from the 11th century onwards. It was not until 1605 that action was taken to regulate the quality of the metal worked and sold, and to protect the public as was done in England. A mark in the form of a lion, a harp and a castle was thenceforward required to be used in addition to another with the device of the maker. Later in the century, in 1637, the Dublin goldsmiths were granted a charter by Charles I, and surviving wares dating from then onwards are found marked with a letter of the alphabet, the initials of the maker, and a crowned harp. From 1730, when a Duty of sixpence an ounce was levied, the figure of Hibernia was stamped in proof of payment. She is shown seated with a harp at her side, and can sometimes be confused with Britannia. Lastly, in 1807 the monarch's head was added to the total.

A further use of a figure of Britannia is less likely to give trouble for two reasons: she is depicted standing and not seated, and the stamp is very rarely seen. It was introduced in England on 1st December 1784 when the payment of duty came into force, and was stamped on articles intended for export so that the maker could claim return of the duty. It proved unsatisfactory because it was used on finished pieces which were unavoidably damaged in being marked, and on 24th July 1785 it ceased to be employed. As it remained current for only eight months and all wares bearing it went overseas, examples of the mark are very rare in England and no more than a half-dozen or so have been recorded.

As mentioned earlier in connexion with London date-letters, the various punches used at the offices in both the capital and the provinces were framed in a number of ways. Oval, square, square with cut-off corners, shield, or rectangular are among the forms that came and went. The

16

London leopard's head appeared sometimes with a crown and sometimes without one, and there were also other minor alterations from time to time. Some of them lasted for no more than a matter of months while others continued in use for years. All can complicate the reading of hallmarks, and make them a matter of argument. On the whole, however, they prove a satisfactory way of both dating a specimen and ensuring it is made of sound metal.

The foregoing is no more than an outline of the system of hallmarking, and can serve only as a rough guide. The best and most thorough book, which illustrates the marks current from year to year and also lists the makers, is *English Goldsmiths and Their Marks*, by Sir Charles James Jackson. It was published first in 1905 and revised and extended in a second edition of 1921. The latter has been reprinted several times and is still obtainable but no alterations have been made to it during the course of the past half-century. A considerable amount of material has been gathered in the period, and one day, no doubt, this will be incorporated in a thoroughly revised version. At the moment, therefore, 'Jackson' remains the standard and indispensable work on the subject.

Less bulky, and adequate for day-to-day purposes, is a small booklet listing marks other than those of makers, which can be bought at most silversmiths for a few shillings.

3. Silverware

Old silverware is one of the more interesting, satisfying and, nowadays, more lucrative objectives of collecting. Of all the applied arts it is one with great adaptability, offering a wide variety of articles which continue to serve useful and decorative purposes. Few people can resist the appearance of the metal, its durability is equally meritorious and its historic place in the esteem of mankind promises for it a lengthy future.

The inherent qualities in silver have assured the preservation of a large quantity. Unlike pottery and porcelain, which are expendable on account of their fragility, silverware is long-lived, and there is a plentiful supply available from which a selection can be made to suit any taste. This applies in particular to the eighteenth century, and explains why it is the subject of the present book.

Great quantities of silver were given or seized during the Civil War, when Royalist and Cromwellian soldiers ranged the countryside. Family plate was 'lent' to either side, and twelve of the Oxford colleges made available for the Cavaliers an amount just short of 20,000 ounces. All of it was melted to provide currency. Succeeding years, although peaceful, did not see a return to such a state of prosperity that the destroyed pieces could be immediately replaced, and silversmiths of the time had a lean existence.

With the restoration of the monarchy in 1660, a very different state of affairs began to prevail. Not only was there a sudden reaction after the

Plate 3   18
(Left to right): skewer. By W. Eley and W. Fearn, 1801. Length 13⅛ inches. Weight 3 oz. 7 dwt.—Sauce ladle. Maker's mark I S, Edinburgh, *circa* 1800. Length 6 inches.—Soup ladle. By Christopher Haines, Dublin, 1774. Length 13¾ inches. Weight 5 oz. 10 dwt.—King's pattern sauce ladle. By J. McKay, Edinburgh, 1851.—Marrow scoop. No maker's mark *cira* 1750. Length 7½ inches.

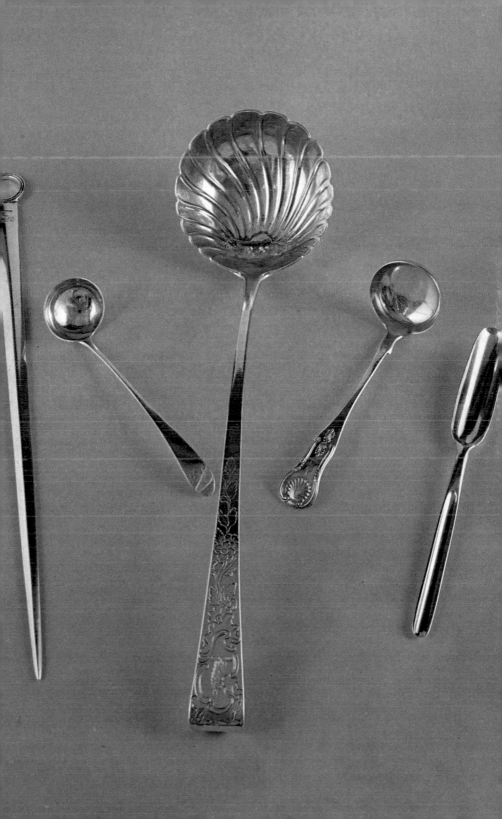

ascetic period of the Commonwealth, but Charles II came from a long sojourn abroad where he had enjoyed the luxury of living in France and Holland. The new King brought with him a liking for comfort and splendour that had been almost forgotten in his native land, and his dutiful subjects made him an annual allowance of £1,300,000 with which he was able to indulge his own tastes and influence theirs.

The ostentation of the Court of Charles II is legendary; the silver bedstead of Nell Gwynne and the silver and gold toilet sets of his other mistresses are only some of the extravagances that were commented on and imitated by the fashionable. Once it had been re-awakened the liking for silverware continued, and by the turn of the century, when William III reigned alone following Mary's death in 1694, the taste was well established.

Fig. 4
Two-handled cup, the body embossed and chased with a running design of flowers and leaves. Maker's mark F L above a bird, 1658. Diameter 5¼ inches.
(*Unless otherwise stated examples illustrated bear London hallmarks*).

Plate 4   19
Teapot with bright cut engraved decoration. By John Emes, 1805. Length 11 inches. Weight 17 oz. 10 dwt. (Left to right): cream jug with embossed and chased decoration. By Thomas Moore, 1751. Height 4¼ inches. Weight 4 oz.—Cream jug decorated with bright cut engraving. By Peter, Ann and William Bateman, 1804. Height 4¾ inches. Weight 3 oz. 10 dwt.

Long before William and Mary had left Holland to become King and Queen of England, there had been plentiful signs of the popularity here of Dutch designs for furniture, brassware and silver. In the case of the first two the productions of each country are sometimes indistinguishable, but the maker's mark on silverware can settle any doubt. Some of the work was that of immigrant craftsmen, but most of it was by Englishmen copying and adapting Dutch pieces or using engraved patterns prepared in Holland.

The commonest type of decoration used in the seventeenth century took the form of embossing and chasing: raised patterns hammered out from the back and front of a piece, respectively, and usually finished with engraved lines and dots. The majority of the designs depict flowers arranged on a matted ground, the most popular subjects being tulips, a relic of the Dutch *Tulpenwoede* (Tulipomania) of 1634 to 1637, and the curly-leaved favourite of the ancient Greeks, the acanthus.

From about 1680, Chinese motifs, copied from those on imported lacquered wares and porcelain, appeared on silver, but after 1700 a change took place. Contrasting with the preceding fussiness there came a reliance on simple, strong shapes with seldom more than an engraved crest or coat of arms to relieve the polished surfaces. A further innovation was the overlaying of parts of an article with shaped sheet silver, the so-called 'cut card' work, which served partly as decoration and partly to strengthen potentially weak areas.

A reason for the lessening Dutch influence was the steady flow of French Huguenot refugees who crossed the Channel in considerable numbers, especially in the last quarter of the seventeenth century. As Protestants in what was a largely Catholic country, they had enjoyed protection under the Edict of Nantes, which had been signed by Henry IV of France in 1598. Under mounting pressure the Protestant churches were closed, and in 1683 there began a series of vicious personal attacks on the Huguenots themselves. Announcing that 'the best of the larger part of our subjects, who formerly held the so-called reformed religion, have embraced the Catholic religion, and therefore the Edict of Nantes has become unnecessary', Louis XIV revoked it. As a result, many thousands of Frenchmen fled the country of their birth and settled in more tolerant lands.

Among the many who came to England were numbers of silversmiths who sought to practise their craft in London. There was an immediate outcry against them from the Goldsmiths', one of their members writing, as early as 1677, in quaint but forcible language:

The poorer sort of Aliens of all sorts of manual Trades, not able to live in their own Country, and others of them of extravagant dispositions, have and do daily come into this Realm . . . do settle at first

20

in private corners, and Garrets, and such like places, and chiefly in the out-parts of this City, and then for their present sustenance, by one means or another, with extraordinary necessitated-diligence, they make Works, and then about with it they go, sometimes to the Gentry, and sometimes to the Native-Tradesmen-Shop-keepers and the same works do sell for less profit than they could afford them, did they live like men. . . .

Fig. 5
Tankard with cut-card work decorating and strengthening the cover and the junctions of the handle and the body. Maker's mark G C, *circa* 1690. Height 6¼ inches. Weight 26 oz.

The author of those words, William Badcock, as both a silversmith and a cutler was doubly open to the threat of under-cutting by the immigrants. He concluded his paragraph with the clear warning: 'observe the ill consequence of suffering these poor Caterpillar-Aliens thus to incroach and undermine us'. Gradually, however, the newcomers overcame the opposition to their arrival, and were accepted by their fellow-workers.

Coming in the main from the provinces of France, most of the Huguenots did not find the prevailing English style as uncongenial as if they had been Parisians. In the capital the fashion was for elaborate ornamentation, and traces of this are sometimes found on important work executed by the immigrants. As in furniture of the times, the first decades of the eighteenth century showed much silver of the plainest design alongside a proportion of examples with sumptuous decoration.

Ornament continued to be embossed and chased, but use was also made of casting. The latter added greatly to the total quantity of metal required for an article, and the careful finishing essential to remove roughness and other signs of the process would also have increased the cost.

The punched work frequently took the form of fluting, with bands of stars and other small-sized motifs centring on a cartouche for the owner's crest or coat of arms. The cartouche, a shaped blank panel owing its name to its origin as a roll of paper or parchment, was surrounded by leafy scrolls and, sometimes, a pattern of fish-scales.

Casting followed the designs associated in France with Jean Bérain, the engraver and draughtsman, and André-Charles Boulle whose furniture was inlaid with brass and tortoiseshell in the manner of Bérain. They made use of straight and curved flat 'strapwork', stiff shell and leaf shapes and female heads. The result often has a chill appearance, but in the hands of some of the best silversmiths, Huguenots like de Lamerie and Platel, it achieves an effect of dignity and richness.

By 1740 a new style altogether had been evolved in France, and quickly found acceptance in England. The rococo (from *rocaille*: rockwork) is based on the natural forms of rocks and seashells and, unlike the formal Bérainesque that preceded it, relied on movement and assymetry. It was popularised, if not introduced, by the French architect and designer, Juste-Aurèle Meissonnier, one of whose commissions was to design a dinner service for the Duke of Kingston. It was made by a French silversmith in 1735, and must have been a first view of the new style for many of those who saw it.

The rococo had its effect not only as regards surface ornament, but is seen in the external shaping of most articles made between about 1740 and 1765. It is coincidental with the so-called 'Chippendale' period of furniture-making, and in many instances the similarity between the broken curves, pie-crust rims and swirling acanthus foliage seen in both mediums is obvious.

Fig. 6
Monteith, gilt, the body fluted and the rim decorated with a cast pattern surmounted by cherub heads. By William Gamble, 1701. Diameter 13 inches. Weight 85 oz.

The Huguenot craftsmen have been credited with introducing and encouraging the style in England, and de Lamerie has been named as its most successful exponent. It is not unreasonable to think that a fashion originating in France should appeal to these men, although many of them were by that time of a generation born in England. Almost all of them employed the rococo with effective results, and while the majority were not innovators they lived mostly in and about Soho where they could easily exchange ideas with one another. English silversmiths adapted themselves to the new style, and it has been shown lately that one of them, in particular, John Edwards, who entered his mark in 1739, executed work of a quality of design and finish comparable to that of any immigrant (See Plate 16 and figs. 50 and 95).

23

Like the contemporaneous cabinet-makers and potters, the silversmiths made use of Chinese motifs. Frequently and appropriately these are seen on tea-caddies, teapots and other objects associated with the popular beverage: temple bells, bewhiskered Chinamen and pagodas all appear as part of the decoration, and are sometimes found placed inconsequentially in European surroundings. Usually they were embossed, and not engraved as they had been at an earlier date.

Fig. 7
Basket with pierced and cast ornament, the swing handle decorated with heads of Chinamen. By S. Herbert and Company, 1756. Width 13¾ inches. Weight about 38 oz.

Although very few pieces bearing his mark are known, those surviving from the workshop of Nicholas Sprimont are noteworthy. He was born at

Liège in 1716 and entered his mark in Goldsmiths' Hall in 1742, between which date and 1747 he is known to have been active as a silversmith. He had a house in Soho, near that of Paul Crespin, also of Continental origin although born in London, and the two men are thought to have collaborated. Sprimont apparently ceased work in 1747 and turned his full attention to manufacturing porcelain at Chelsea. Here, he became manager, and between 1758 and 1769 was the sole proprietor.

Both Sprimont and Crespin were typical of several other men of their time, in that they produced designs of surprising inventiveness. Thus, a soup-tureen, of which a drawing by Sprimont is in the Victoria and Albert Museum, shows it with supports straddled by ostriches and with a large artichoke as a knob for the cover. Likewise, a large tureen made by Crespin in 1740, now in the museum at Toledo, Ohio, is formed of two seated goats supporting a bowl and cover surmounted by an assortment of modelled fruit.

Fig. 8
Tureen and cover in the form of two seated goats supporting a bowl of fruit. By Paul Crespin, 1740. Width 21¾ inches. Weight 524 oz.

25

These and other pieces have been criticised as 'ponderous', and the entire style was once castigated as 'vulgar'. Fashions change, and each generation eschews that of its predecessors, so by 1760, when the rococo had held sway for a full twenty years, the time was ripe for something fresh.

A reaction began to set in against the curves inseparable from rococo; the assymetry, the rockwork and the shells were swept away. In place of them came straight lines and decorative motifs harking back to classical Greece and Rome, which were rendered with a geometrical precision completely opposite to the naturalism of recently favoured forms.

The new style, known as the neo-classical, had been developing for some years in France, and came briskly to the fore at about the time when the Scottish architect, Robert Adam, returned in 1758 from a three-year tour of the Mediterranean area. Prior to setting up in practice in London he had been spending a portion of his time when abroad in measuring and drawing remains of the past. He had also made the acquaintance of some of the leading artists and innovators in both Italy and France. Although it was in the latter country that the new mode first gained a hold, by the early 1760's wealthy Englishmen had begun to adopt it.

The general public, no less than scholars, were intrigued by excavations which had been begun to uncover the remains of Pompeii, near Naples. Commenced in 1758, they were reported on and illustrated throughout Europe during the ensuing years, and were a factor in the rejection of rococo.

Much of the credit for the acceptance of the new forms was due to the skill and energy of Josiah Wedgwood, whose newly-developed types of pottery were acclaimed far and wide. Not only did he produce wares different in composition from any made before, but he modelled them in shapes founded on those of the ancients or of a simplicity that was admired, bought and imitated.

Probably the most noticeable feature of much silver of the years after 1770 is that hollow wares, such as tea and other pots, jugs and cups were raised on a pedestal foot and their bodies, which formerly had tended to be globular, became elongated. The silhouette which had been squat grew tall and narrow, and handles tended to stretch upwards rather than outwards. Ornament was confined mostly to chains of husks tied by ribbons and centred on round and oval discs known as *paterae*. The Grecian honeysuckle-like *anthemion* was also much employed, and the acanthus leaf continued in undiminished popularity.

Both embossing and engraving were used, and a variant of the latter, known as 'bright cut' work, was introduced. It somewhat resembles chiselling, with shaped cuts which glittered and gave it its name. Although

26

Fig. 9
Sugar basket, the boat-shaped body
raised on a pedestal foot and decorated
with festoons in bright cut engraving.
By Hester Bateman, 1785.

27

it was not confined to any one maker or area, the Birmingham manufacturers were particularly fond of using bright cut decoration and it is sometimes regarded as a distinctive feature of anchor-stamped pieces. It is at its most attractive on the handles of spoons of various kinds, and proved highly suitable for rendering the feminine traceries of fashionable design in the 30 or so years after 1775.

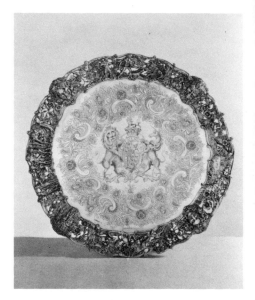

Fig. 10
Gilt tray with a cast rim, engraved border and central coat of arms of Adolphus Frederick, Duke of Cambridge, son of George III. Maker's mark EM, 1825.Diameter 25½ inches. Weight 273 oz.

Throughout the century the majority of silverware was left to shine in its natural colour, but a proportion of pieces was given a coating of pure gold. When completely covered with it a piece is described as 'silver-gilt', but when the gold is used only in selected areas it is termed 'parcel-gilt'. In addition to enhancing the appearance of an article, the gilding also prevented tarnishing, or at least slowed its course, and it was also very much cheaper to have something of silver-gilt than in solid gold. The latter, also, was not always a practical proposition as the metal itself was nearly twice as heavy as silver, and large-sized objects made from it would be unmanageable.

Size, however, would seem not to have been considered a handicap in the case of much of the silverware of the first quarter of the nineteenth century. In a book published in 1806, Charles Heathcote Tatham, an architect and designer, clearly stated what was to be a guiding principle for many years to come. He noted: '. . . instead of Massiveness, the principal character of good Plate, light and insignificant forms have prevailed, to the utter exclusion of all good Ornament whatsoever.'

28

Fig. 11
'. . . . Massiveness, the principal character
of good Plate . . .'. Gilt candelabrum in
the form of Hercules slaying the Hydra.
By Edward Farrell, 1824–25. Height 35
inches. Weight 1144 oz.

From that time much silver and silver-gilt is remarkable for the scale on which it was made, and the profusion of ornament it bears. As with Regency furniture, many types of design were incorporated to provide a wide selection for the purchaser. Greek and Roman, Egyptian, French and Chinese; all contributed to the creation of objects ranging from cups to candlesticks.

4. Silverware (ii)

The custom of engraving a crest or coat of arms on a piece of plate was common throughout the eighteenth century and earlier, and continues to the present day. Where it is certain that such work is contemporary with the article it adorns it can serve as a handy confirmation of date. Wear and general signs of age affect engraving, as anything else, and it is usually not difficult to detect if it is modern. Occasionally, however, a crest or coat can have been added a decade or two after manufacture, and is less obvious. A knowledge of the styles employed over the years will assist in this direction.

While the full understanding of a coat or crest is the province of a genealogist, the mantling, or ornament surrounding the shield, can be informative. In the last half of the seventeenth century it was often in the form of a number of plumes or palm leaves, drawn in a series of almost parallel lines, the ends crossed and tied with a ribbon. Occasionally the representation was so formalised as to make recognition difficult, but in other instances there can be no doubt about what the engraver portrays (see Figs. 34 and 57).

In the succeeding years, when designs were influenced by the Frenchman Bérain, feathers and leaves remained a feature, but were accompanied by flat strapwork arranged in scrolling patterns. Exceptionally, when other engraved work was involved, the mantling was designed to incorporate elements appearing elsewhere on the article, and the whole formed a unified composition.

31

The imbalance of rococo design is reflected very clearly in the mantling coming into use in the early 1740's, and current for the next two to three decades. Plumes and palm-leaves were no longer employed, and their place was taken by elaborate curves interspersed with flowering branches and shell-like shapes. The shield, which had hitherto been regular in outline, now became uneven to match the general appearance of the whole subject.

Fig. 12
Tray with 'Pie-crust' rim and a central engraved coat of arms. By John Robinson, 1744. Diameter 6½ inches.

The last thirty years of the eighteenth century saw a gradual decline in the use of mantling, with the regularly-shaped shield returning to favour. It was drawn sometimes suspended from tied ribbons, but was often completely without embellishment.

There were numerous exceptions to the styles noted above, and it is to be noted that whereas the earlier arms were drawn very simply the later ones had more detail. From after 1700 increasing trouble was taken to render the various colours of the heraldic devices by means of lines and dots. The code used was the following:

Gold (*or*)	Dots
Silver (*argent*)	Plain white
Red (*gules*)	Vertical lines
Blue (*azure*)	Horizontal lines
Black (*sable*)	Vertical lines crossing horizontal ones
Green (*vert*)	Diagonal lines, from top left
Purple (*purpure*)	Diagonal lines, from top right

A considerable quantity of silverware exists bearing the Royal coat of arms with the familiar supporters of a lion and a unicorn at either side. At one time it was supposed that all such pieces had once been owned by the Kings and Queens of England, but this is not the case. Most of them are what are now referred to as 'Ambassadorial Plate', because they were once in the possession of ambassadors or other persons appointed to important positions.

When an ambassador was sent from England in order that, in the words of Sir Henry Wotton, he might 'lie abroad for the good of his country', it was deemed that he should represent his sovereign in a worthy manner. To that end it became usual for the Royal Jewel Office to lend him a suitable quantity of silverware, each piece bearing on it the Royal arms of its true owner. By the early years of the eighteenth century it had become customary for this to be looked upon as a perquisite of office, and the silver, valued at anything between £2,000 and £3,000 was treated as an outright gift.

In addition to envoys, the Speaker of the House of Commons and the Lord Chancellor were among the small and select group of officials enjoying the same privilege. In most instances the silver took the form of a dinner service, so that a suitable impression of the importance of the occasion might be conveyed to visitors. Thus, when Sir John Cust was elected Speaker of the House of Commons in 1761 he was supplied with a large dinner-service from the Jewel House. Each piece was engraved with the arms of George III, the Garter motto (*Honi soit qui mal y pense*), a crown and

the Royal cypher, *G.R.*, and the whole, which included a set of 8 candlesticks, weighed a total of over 2,000 oz. When he was re-elected to the
office in the following Parliament, Sir John was able to draw a further
quantity of silver from the same source. (See DINNER SERVICES,
page 83).

Fig. 13
Knives, spoons and forks engraved with
the Royal crown, the cypher of George I
and the Garter motto, part of the plate
issued to Paul Methuen on his appoint-
ment in 1714 as ambassador to Spain. By
George Lambe and other makers, 1714.

Finally, by 1815 the custom had become abused to such a degree that
action was taken to end it. Viscount Castlereagh, the foreign minister at
the time, ordered that each embassy should be issued with its own silverware,
which remained part of the contents of the building to do duty for successive

Plate 5   34
Hot water jug, the body and cover partly reeded. By S. Hennell and J. Taylor, 1814. Height 8¾
inches. Weight 21 oz. (all in).

occupants. However, the claims of others than ambassadors to the perquisite remained undisturbed for years, and the Speaker did not lose his until 1839.

While the majority of ware with the Royal arms was obtained in this manner, a certain amount was made to the order of a sovereign for presentation to deserving subjects and foreign notabilities. Other pieces came on the market in 1808 due to the financial troubles of the Prince Regent, who was then making serious attempts to rid himself of his wife. He arranged for her to live separately in Kensington Palace, but while the Treasury were agreeable to paying for suitable furniture they objected to providing £5,440 for silverware.

It was thought that the Jewel Office might be able to loan some, but the answer was that they possessed nothing fit for the purpose. However, they did suggest handing over a quantity of old pieces, which was 'neither available for service in its present form nor valuable from its antiquity or workmanship'. The permission of George III was given, and the pieces were sent to the Royal silversmiths, Rundell, Bridge and Rundell, to be melted to defray some of the cost of new articles.

The firm followed its own inclinations and business instincts in the matter, and instead of consigning their purchases to the furnace they sold them as they were. All bore Royal insignia, and some that have re-appeared on the market in recent years have been traced to old inventories of the contents of St. James's Palace and other residences.

Those who had not been granted, or who preferred not to use, a coat of arms, were often content simply to put their initials on their possessions. For much of the seventeenth and eighteenth centuries a married couple arranged them in a triangle. Usually thus: J S M, for John and Mary Smith; with the surname above the initials of husband and wife. Most often such a mark of ownership was engraved on the underside of a piece, along with the 'scratched weight' (see page 7).

An inscription recording the gift of a piece can often prove historically interesting as well as provide confirmation of the date of manufacture. Presentations to God-children are frequently dated, as are the names of winning race-horses and their owners; all traditionally the recipients of silverware on auspicious occasions.

Trophies were, and still are, presented to winners of all kinds of contests, and the architect Robert Adam was not above designing racing cups. One of them, awarded at Richmond, Yorkshire, in 1770 is of two-handled classical form, chased with acanthus leaves and with a frieze and panels of racehorses. Most renowned in recent years of all such articles is the solid gold teapot given by George II in 1736 at Leith races, in Scotland. It was won by a black mare named 'Legacy', owned by a Mr Croft, and then vanished until 1847. In that year a London silversmith sold it to a private buyer for £70,

Plate 6   35
Nutmeg grater. By Hester Bateman, 1787. Length 3¼ inches. Weight 1 oz. 10 dwt. (all in).—
Double-opening snuff box. By J. Taylor, Birmingham, 1808. Length 2¾ inches. Weight 2 oz.—
Apple corer, see Plate 11.

and it again went into hiding for about a century. Then, in 1940 it was sold by auction at Christie's and realised £1,250. It made newspaper headlines when it re-appeared in the same saleroom in December 1967 to fetch no less than £40,000 ($96,000, see fig. 86, page 147).

Engraved coats of arms and crests enhance the appearance of silver, but embossing and chasing added at a later date only very rarely succeed in achieving this. It has been widely acknowledged that the distinguishing feature of most eighteenth century English silver is its good, but simple, design. In particular, the tankards, coffee-pots, teapots and other pieces with plain lines give the qualities of the metal every opportunity to be seen at their best. The shining smooth surfaces epitomise the malleability and strength of the material, which has a quality described by Alexander Pope as 'soft splendour'.

Although such pieces have been among the most highly esteemed for the past quarter of a century, this was not always the case. In the years around 1850 they were unfashionable and despised; uncluttered purity of line had no place amid furniture and china overloaded with carved or moulded ornament of every variety. To sell the rejected articles and buy new was not such an economic proposition as it had been in the past, and if this was done it was the exception rather than the rule. Instead, recourse was had to adding suitable decoration by embossing and chasing old pieces.

Judging by the very large quantity of examples still extant, the work must have been carried out on a considerable scale. It is possible that only a few firms catered for it, and that they did the work submitted by silversmiths from all over the country. There appears to be no record of who these specialists were, and if their identities could be discovered at least a black mark could be put against their names.

Most of the new work was a pastiche of rococo; with scrolls, flowers, and other elements of the style forming a passable imitation of the real thing. In most instances there is a clearly discernible stiffness about the curves to betray the copyist, and the whole lacks the flow and movement given to it by an eighteenth century craftsman. Little less popular than rococo, was early Georgian, which was applied in the form of straight or spiral flutes and a clumsy cartouche.

While it is not always as simple as it sounds to recognise the work of a later hand, the more obvious anachronisms cannot fail to attract notice. Thus, it is not unusual to find work in the early Georgian manner, normally current in about 1720, on an article date-stamped 1750. More often, however, one sees rococo ornament of the type current in Chippendale's heyday (c. 1760), on pieces of much earlier make. In these cases suspicions are aroused and a critical look at the pattern will show what has happened.

Fig. 14
Tankard. By Thomas Bevault, 1714.
Height 7 inches. Weight 23 oz. 19 dwt.
The embossed and chased decoration
added at a later date.

Fig. 15
Tankard or mug. By Thomas Whipham,
1748. Height 4¾ inches. Weight 13 oz.
10 dwt. The embossed and chassed decoration added at a later date.

Additional embossing and chasing did not entail re-assaying or, perhaps more important, payment of duty. In modern eyes the work has ruined much of the appeal of pieces on which it appears, and their financial value is likewise affected. The ornament can be removed by careful hammering, but this is likely to result in distortion of the article and probably one or more thin spots where the impressions were deep. To hide traces of this having been performed, recourse is had to electro-plating. It covers the whole piece with a coating of silver, levels most of the inequalities and usually leaves the surface with a new-looking glitter.

Alterations, however, which result in a change in the overall appearance or function of a piece of silver, or involve the addition of a portion weighing more than a quarter of the whole, mean that it must be hall-marked again. Under an Act of 1844 it should be treated in the same manner as an entirely new article. Alternatively, if the extra portion weighs under twenty-five per cent of the original then only the new part need be assayed and marked.

Over the years, certain kinds of silverware have been prone to suffer such transformations. They were carried out in order to convert what were then unsaleable articles into others more acceptable to buyers of the time. For this reason a small-sized tankard was given a V-shaped cut in the front of the rim, and with a suitable piece of metal soldered in the gap it became a cream jug. Teapots have been shorn of handles and spouts to convert them into tea-caddies, and spoons have been painstakingly filed and hammered to emerge as much rarer forks.

Equally fraudulent are small articles, especially spoons, cast from old ones. In most instances the marks are blurred and reveal the process by which the object has been made; there is an unmistakable sharpness about a hall-mark that has been stamped in the regular manner with a steel punch. Also, casting is only very rarely completely successful, and a strong glass will show pitting and minute broken bubbles that should not be present.

The most unscrupulous of all deceptions involve the falsification of genuine hall-marks by partially 'wearing' one or more of them so as to render them undecipherable and suggest the piece is older than it really is. The lion's head and Britannia when used on higher standard metal after 1719 offers a temptation to alter marks so that an article with them appears to fall within the period 1697–1720. There have also been modern attempts in the manner of the old 'duty dodgers'; cutting out the marked portion of a commonplace article and carefully inserting it in a later or completely new one. Surgery of this nature is usually revealed by breathing hard on the area around the marks, when the line of solder will be revealed.

The actual placing of marks on their work by the old makers varied from man to man and from decade to decade. By and large they did obey what might be termed unwritten rules, and these were summarised by Sir Charles

Jackson fifty years ago. His notes constitute no more than a very rough guide or, as he called them 'hints':

> Marks are rarely found hidden in the bottom of an article of earlier date than the latter part of the seventeenth century. Early tankards are generally marked on the drum to the right of the handle and across the cover. Later ones with domed tops, as well as cups, casters, tea vases, tea and coffee pots, are for the most part marked under the base out of view, and the covers of later tankards are generally marked inside the dome.

The phrase 'generally marked' occurs twice in the preceding paragraph, and there are a surprising number of exceptions to be found.

Fig. 16
Tankard with cast thumbpiece, flat-topped domed lid and moulded base, the body with formal acanthus leaf decoration and the lid with flowers and leaves. Hallmarked on top of lid and side of body; maker's mark R N crowned, 1678. Height 8¼ inches. Weight 42 oz. 2 dwt.

Strictly speaking each separate part of an article should bear a full set of marks, but sometimes only the main body does so. The hinged covers of tankards and other lidded containers are sometimes found bearing only the Sterling lion. Occasionally, also, articles bear the mark of more than one maker. This is not uncommon with handled ware; such things as fish slices often having the blade by one man and the handle by another. Doubtless certain silversmiths specialised in making the latter, and supplied them ready-marked. A maker's mark is also found sometimes obliterating, or semi-obliterating, that of another. Usually this is the result of a retailer, who had entered his own mark, over-stamping that of the actual maker.

Forgers very rarely succeed completely in their deceitful task, and something can almost always be relied on to give them away. If they are clumsy, then a lack of skill is evident; if they are good craftsmen, then their own personalities creep in somewhere and give their work a subtle touch of modernity. Only experience enables a dealer or collector to give judgement in doubtful cases, and in some instances no two opinions will agree.

Undoubtedly the collector is protected to the fullest degree if he or she relies on the reasoned advice of a reputable dealer or the cataloguing of a first-class auction-room. In the latter event, important lots often list former owners, who can have been respected connoisseurs and thus imply a guarantee of the genuineness of the piece. A good dealer will always willingly commit his opinion to writing, and a clearly-worded receipt is a reassuring document and a valuable one in case of later dispute.

5. The Silversmiths

We know surprisingly little about the organisation of many old crafts, but recently-awakened interest is slowly providing a clearer picture of conditions a couple of centuries ago. It was once accepted, for instance, that the name on a clock face was quite certainly that of the man who had made the mechanism. Now it is agreed that clock-making was a well-organised trade, and that a majority of the names are those of men who retailed goods made elsewhere. Many of them did little more than assemble parts bought from others who specialised in making particular items of the mechanism. Likewise, the cases were made by cabinet-makers who concentrated on providing them.

By about the same date, the mid-eighteenth century, silversmithing was on a comparable footing, and a maker's mark does not invariably indicate that he actually produced the piece bearing it. There had been a degree of specialisation before this, when such men as Simon Gribelin, who came to England from France a few years prior to 1685, worked at engraving the backs of watches and the delicate cocks protecting the balance and its spring, as well as decorating silver in the same fashion.

In order to carry on a business in London it was essential for a man to belong to one of the City Companies, and Gribelin became a member of the Clockmakers'. His engraving on silver is very finely executed, and a few examples are signed with his initials. He died in 1733 some years after an English born rival, William Hogarth, had completed his apprenticeship.

Hogarth, who later became famous as a painter in oils, was apprenticed to a silversmith, Ellis Gamble of Cranbourn Street, Leicester Square, whose trade-card he engraved. Of his work on silver the most important and imposing is the large rectangular salver, 'The Walpole Salver', now in the Victoria and Albert Museum. It was made in 1727–28 by Paul de Lamerie to the order of the Chancellor of the Exchequer of the time, Sir Robert Walpole. A perquisite of the latter's office was the silver Exchequer seal which became obsolete on the death of the monarch, in this instance George I, and was melted down to provide metal for the salver.

The seals of William III and Queen Anne had been similarly converted into salvers engraved by Simon Gribelin who, at the age of 66, might have been considered too old, or infirm to undertake the third in his lifetime. That Hogarth actually did engrave it has been disputed from time to time but it is more often attributed to him than not. One of the points in favour of his authorship is the fact that he engraved the coat of arms of de Lamerie, which is known from a print taken from it. The work was probably executed on a piece of silver, doubtless made by the master-silversmith, which has unfortunately disappeared.

The maker's mark really means that the owner of it was responsible for having the piece assayed, and that it was up to his standard of quality in all respects. Whether he was the real maker is another matter and cannot always be decided with certainty. It must be sufficient that a number of names are associated with outstanding craftsmanship and having been famed in their own day, as they still are, it was inevitable that they should have been overburdened with work. Naturally they would have accepted all the orders that came their way, and to fulfil them they sub-contracted to other silversmiths. A similar state of affairs occurred in the pottery industry, as when Josiah Wedgwood supplied figures he had had made by a neighbouring firm, but which were stamped clearly WEDGWOOD.

What we do know about the eighteenth century silversmiths is principally names, addresses and dates, with very little indeed to instil a breath of life into the shadowy figures. Of the most famed of all of them, Paul de Lamerie, who has been the subject of a book devoted entirely to his life and work, it is about the latter that we have the majority of information. We know that he was in England by 1691 when he was three years old, having been brought by his parents from Holland. They made their home in Berwick Street, Soho, and when he was 15 the boy was apprenticed to a Huguenot silversmith, Pierre Platel.

He became a member of the Goldsmiths' Company in 1712, and entered his mark in that year. His surviving work shows consistently high quality in design and execution, and in most instances the amount of metal employed proves that he worked for wealthy patrons. When Admiral Lord Anson

43

received his share of the prize-money from his successful exploit in capturing a galleon (see page 2), it made him a rich man overnight and for a supply of silverware befitting his new status he went to de Lamerie.

Fig. 17
Caster with octagonal body and pierced and engraved top. By Paul de Lamerie, 1724. Height 9 inches. Weight 25 oz. 13 dwt.

Between 1712 and 1751 when he died, Paul de Lamerie's work followed the various styles that came and went over the years. While some of it is heavily decorated much is simple in appearance but of outstandingly correct design. Few makers have produced so many pieces of which the proportions and details of each are so generally acceptable today.

Men who specialised in certain processes, such as engraving, have been mentioned but there were also silversmiths who produced a steady flow of certain articles. For instance, the mark of Robert Abercromby, who flourished from about 1730 to 1755, is so often found on salvers that it may be doubted if he made anything else. Likewise John Cafe and William Cafe produced pairs and sets of candlesticks between about 1740 and 1780, and William Eley, with and without partners, concentrated his energies between about 1780 and 1810 on small plate: spoons and forks of all kinds.

It is difficult to name anyone who immediately succeeded de Lamerie as a supplier of wares of a distinctively high quality, but perhaps John Schofield deserves mention in this connexion. There were, however, very many silversmiths in business in the second half of the century whose work was good but not brilliant, and this was due to the fact that a few wealthy patrons had been replaced by a large number of moderately rich ones. The latter did not demand, and probably could not afford, the finest wares and were content with something less.

Fig. 18
Candelabrum, the upper arms (or branch) removable so that it may be used as a candlestick. By John Schofield, 1793. Height 22¼ inches.

Typical of those supplying goods in this category were the Bateman family, who have received considerable attention from collectors in recent years. This is accounted for partly because their workmanship was competent, the designs were attractive and, perhaps because the head of the firm and of the family was a woman, Hester, and this fact has caught the public imagination. She was the widow of John Bateman who had a business in Bunhill Row, between Old Street and Chiswell Street, in the City, and who died in 1760. At that date Hester was fifty-one, but she would seem to have been a determined and business-like woman who set about ensuring the future prosperity of her children by continuing and expanding the existing silversmithing business. She entered her mark in 1761, and from then until her retirement in 1790, at the age of 81, her initials in script characters appeared on a wide range of articles.

The silver made by members of the Bateman family, particularly that with Hester's mark on it, shares the thin elegance of many productions of the period. The classical vase forms are ornamented with cast beaded borders and with gentle ovals and meandering garlands in bright cut engraving. Writing in 1785, Horace Walpole referred scathingly to 'Mr Adam's gingerbread and sippets of embroidery' but many people, now as in the past, admire the style and do not share the opinion of the Sage of Strawberry Hill. While it has been suggested that Hester's use of such decorative motifs reflects a feminine mind, this is no more than wishful hindsight as she was not by any means alone in their employment.

Fig. 19
Jewish Sabbath-lamp, the top section decorated with paterae and swags of drapery in the neo-classical taste. By Hester Bateman, 1787. Height 35½ inches. Weight 54 oz. 17 dwt.

The fact that a woman carried on a business when she became widowed was no phenomenon in the eighteenth century or later. It was Alice

Hepplewhite who published her late husband's book of designs, *The Cabinet-maker and Upholsterer's Guide*, two years after she had become a widow. The title page named her firm as A. Hepplewhite and Co., and there are innumerable instances throughout the century of women in business. Whether Mrs Hepplewhite handled a plane or chisel, or Mrs Bateman a hammer or graver are different matters, and it is possible that both spent their time in the counting-house rather than at the work-bench.

However, it cannot be assumed that in either instance the head of the firm had no say in what was made by the craftsmen they employed. Whether Hester Bateman or an anonymous manager decided the shapes and patterns to be followed is unknown and probably will never be discovered, but there is often a close similarity between the productions of her firm and those of her contemporaries. Their inspiration must have had a common source, and each would have owed something to the work of the others.

The opening of assay offices in Birmingham and Sheffield in 1773 was due primarily to the efforts of Matthew Boulton. For some years he had been making metal wares at his Soho works, just outside Birmingham, and had turned to silver in about 1765. For assaying he had to send his goods either to London, Chester or York, which were 112, 72 and 125 miles distant. Delays and damage could result, as they had done when Boulton wrote to the Earl of Shelbourne in 1771 about the twelve days in which some candlesticks had been away at Chester for marking.

Not only was the chasing 'entirely destroyed' and a week needed for repairs, but, he continued:

I am so exceedingly vex'd about the disappointment and loss which have attended the two pairs of candlesticks that altho' I am very desirous of becoming a great Silversmith, yet I am determined never to take up that branch in the Large Way I intended unless powers can be obtained to have a Marking Hall at Birmingham. This is not the first time by several that I have been served so. I had one parcel of Candlesticks quite broke by their careless packing.

As Lord Shelburne was a prominent politician this was skilful lobbying on Boulton's part, but no doubt there was an element of truth in his tale of misfortune.

The first piece of silver to be marked at the Birmingham office has all the characteristics of Boulton's work. It is a tea-urn, now in Birmingham City Museum and Art Gallery, and was the first item to be entered on the Plate Register when Boulton sent 841 oz. of ware to be assayed on 31st August 1773. The urn is of simple classical shape with upward curving handles modelled with leaves at each end, the body and cover are partly fluted and the whole stands on a square pedestal raised on four foliate feet.

47

Fig. 20
Candlestick with embossed and chased
gadrooning and acanthus leaves. By
Matthew Boulton, 1813. Height 13
inches.

Matthew Boulton was in the forefront of the Industrial Revolution, and foresaw that mass-production would increase sales and profits while benefiting mankind, but he learned from experience that the same rule did not apply to the making of articles requiring more than a minimum of hand workmanship. Steam-power, made available through his partnership with James Watt, was applicable only to a limited number of silversmithing operations, and it was found hard to compete with the London makers who had longer experience and were at the seat of fashion. Boulton's productions were stamped with his initials together with those of another partner, John Fothergill, but in 1782 the latter died and then MB alone was used. Whether with one or both marks, the wares remain in high favour with collectors.

The transport conditions of the day meant that most provincial communities were comparatively isolated from the capital. As a result, the farther distant they lay from it, the longer the time-lag between the introduction of a style or variation in London and its adoption elsewhere. This state of affairs was more noticeable at the beginning of the century than at the end, and in places like York and Exeter they commonly made pieces in fashions outmoded in London a decade or more earlier. For this reason the more up to date country dwellers equipped their homes with silver and furniture from the capital city, and relied on local makers only for their minor requirements.

Although Boulton's success with silverware was perhaps less spectacular than he hoped, his fellow-citizens in the 'toy' trade were able to take full advantage of the newly-opened assay-office. Birmingham had for long been the centre of manufacture of small-sized articles of all kinds, which were known in the eighteenth century as 'toys' and which we would call 'trifles'. Such things as shoe buckles, small boxes for all purposes, and watch chains were made at first from copper and brass and then from silver. In the case of the latter, the initials of Thomas Willmore, Samuel Pemberton and Joseph Taylor, among others, are found on many such articles.

They constituted a considerable proportion of Birmingham's output, while in London the more luxurious wares, of a kind rarely seen since the earlier years of the century began to be in demand. The man whose name is most closely associated with their making, Paul Storr, was the subject of a book written by the late Dr N. M. Penzer, who sub-titled the volume 'The last of the goldsmiths'. However, in view of the awakening interest in, and appreciation of, the work of Victorian makers, this is beginning to prove less acceptable than it seemed in 1954 when the book was published.

Born in 1771, Storr was apprenticed in 1785 to a Swedish-born silversmith, Andrew Fogelberg of Church Street, Soho, and during a short period in partnership with William Frisbee he entered his mark in 1793.

Three years later he was in business on his own in Air Street, off Regent Street and close to Piccadilly Circus, where he remained until 1807. After that year he appeared in directories under the entry:

Storr & Co. Working Silversmiths 53, Dean Street, Soho.

Fig. 21
Teapot. By Paul Storr, 1795, two years after he had entered his mark at Goldsmiths' Hall. Height 6 inches. Weight 14 oz. 16 dwt. (all in: including wood knob and handle).

He had returned to within a short distance of where he had been apprenticed, and was busily engaged in fulfilling orders received by the eminent firm of Royal silversmiths, Rundell, Bridge & Rundell, of Ludgate Hill.

Philip Rundell was the son of a doctor near Bath, and after serving an apprenticeship with a jeweller he took employment in about 1767 with a firm of jewellers and silversmiths in London. After some fifteen years, in which he learned the retail side of the trade and served customers, Rundell bought out his employer and carried on the business under his own name. In 1777 another assistant had been taken on, John Bridge, from Dorset, and 11 years later he became Rundell's partner.

Plate 7   50
Pair of sauce boats with leaf-capped scroll handles and palmate feet. By George Hunter, *circa* 1755. Length 7¾ inches. Weight 19 oz. 5 dwt.

Bridge was an astute business man, and his cousin, who farmed success-fully in Dorset came to the notice of the King, whose deep interest in agricultural matters had earned him the title of 'Farmer George'. As a result of the Dorset John Bridge mentioning his Ludgate Street relative it was not very long before Messrs. Rundell and Bridge held warrants as suppliers to the King and Queen as well as to other members of the Royal family. By 1804 they had been joined by Rundell's nephew, who brought them additional capital.

Of the two elder partners, Philip Rundell was described as being 'very sly and cunning, and suspicious in the extreme', was a thoroughly un-pleasant-tempered man who lived meanly and left one and a half million pounds when he died in 1827. Bridge was altogether different in character, and the reason for some (or most) of his business success is clear from a description written of him in the early 1840s. It was the work of an old employee who united a discerning eye with a nimble pen, and left this picture for posterity.

. . . although he possessed as much Pride as any Person need have yet to any one and to every one by whom he expected to gain any thing he was apparently the most humble and obedient Person that could well be imagined, his back was exceedingly flexible and no man in London could bow lower or oftener than could Mr. Bridge. In fact he was a complete Courtier and was highly respected in the Palaces of Princes, and the Halls of Servants, for his great humility in the former, and his great condescension in the latter. He well knew it was of great im-portance to him to stand well with all the Servants in a great House and he had learnt (as he often confessed it) that the nearest way to My Lady's Boudoir was down the Area Steps through the Servant's Hall and from thence to the Housekeepers Room and so up stairs to my Lady.

After a dozen years of working for the Ludgate Hill firm, Storr broke away, opened a workshop in Clerkenwell and was once more free to please himself in what he made and who he supplied. Finally he became partner in a retail business in Bond Street, under the style of Storr and Mortimer. Paul Storr retired in 1839, and five years later, at the age of 73, he died and was buried in Tooting.

Storr's workmanship is invariably of the highest quality, and in design it ranges from the most elaborate to pieces of a Scandinavian simplicity. While this proves he was able to work in a variety of styles, it leaves un-answered the question of whether he played a large or a small part in designing his output. It is known that Rundell and Bridge employed John Flaxman and William Theed, the sculptors, to plan important pieces, and other artists were also involved. Storr did not, therefore, initiate such

Plate 8   51
Pair of coasters with pierced galleries. By Edward Lowe, 1776. Diameter $4\frac{7}{8}$ inches.—Wine label lettered PORT. By Joseph Wilson, 1800.—Wine label lettered SHERRY. Unmarked, *circa* 1790.

productions, which is not to denigrate him as a straightforward craftsman but means that he had no responsibility for the design.

His predecessors possibly played a similar role, but until evidence is forthcoming, one way or the other, uncertainty will remain. In Storr's case, a book of drawings in the Victoria and Albert Museum (discussed and illustrated by Mr Charles Oman in an article in *Apollo* magazine, March 1966) is related to some of the work he executed for Rundells. It is suggested that they were adaptations of ideas by Theed and others into practical form for the silversmith. Comparable designs were doubtless prepared throughout the century for other silversmiths, whose task was not to originate forms but to translate the flat sketch into a reality in the round. How well they succeeded can be seen in many of the examples illustrated in this book.

Fig. 22
Tureen and cover ornamented with gadrooning and formal shells, the handles reeded and springing from lion masks. By Paul Storr, 1809. Width 17⅜ inches. Weight 220 oz.

A Dictionary of Silver Articles

APPLE CORERS

These small and useful instruments were made throughout the century, but most surviving examples date from the years after 1790. The majority of them are made so that the curved cutting blade can be unscrewed, and when reversed fits inside the hollow handle. In this way the instrument could be safely carried in a pocket or purse, as it was doubtless intended for use on open-air occasions. Some of the early examples have a compartment for spice in the handle. See plates 6 and 11.

ARGYLLS

The Argyll, which is sometimes spelt Argyle, owes its name to one of the Dukes of Argyll. There has been disagreement over which of these Scottish noblemen gave the object its name, but most probably it was Archibald, third Duke of Argyll, who was born in 1682 and succeeded to the title on the death of his brother in 1743. He died in 1761.

The purpose of the Argyll is to keep gravy warm at the dinner table, and it does this either by means of hot water contained in an inner liner or by a heated piece of iron similarly jacketed. In shape the majority of the vessels resemble teapots, but a spectacular example standing nearly 14 inches in height, at Queen's College, Oxford, is in the form of a two-handled vase which appears to present no means of removing its contents. The water-filled variety have external filling orifices with small hinged

53

covers and, unlike teapots, the principal cover is usually completely removable instead of being hinged.

The earliest recorded example is dated 1755, and they continued to be made in the first half of the 19th century. Their shapes and ornament followed prevailing styles, but they were doubtless made only in small numbers as they are comparatively scarce. According to Mr Harold Newman, who has studied them in detail, they find a use in America for coffee and hot milk and modern reproductions are made for the purpose.

ASPARAGUS TONGS

Tongs for serving asparagus were first made towards the end of the eighteenth century. The most commonly-found type is of somewhat later date, with a pair of flat, square-ended blades, grooved inside to grip the vegetable. They are rounded at the handle to work like a pair of sugar tongs.

Fig. 23
Basket with shaped panels of pierced ornament. By Thomas Heming, 1762. Width 16 inches.

54

BASKETS

Baskets for holding bread took a number of forms during the eighteenth century. The majority of them were oval in outline, and almost all have their sides pierced with a pattern or are fashioned in imitation of woven wicker. Exceptional examples take the form of a large-sized seashell, with a single upcurved handle. Most of the baskets dating from the first decades of the century have a handle projecting at each end, while those of later date have a hinged handle which falls flat along the rim of the article for storage.

The basket-weave type has an attractive simplicity, but the extravagance of the rococo style lent itself particularly well to the ornamentation of many of those made in the mid-century. Typical of them is one bearing the mark of S. Herbert & Co., entered at Goldsmiths' Hall in 1750 (see fig. 7, page 24).The sloping sides are pierced in an Oriental pattern bordered with raised scrolls and shells, the four short feet are linked by an apron matching the rim, and the swing handle and base are modelled with small busts of Chinamen.

BEAKERS

The shape of the beaker goes back to medieval times, and probably earlier. It has been suggested it is owed to the use of a section of animal's horn having been cut for conversion into a drinking vessel. To this it would owe its shape of straight sides sloping outwards from a circular base.

Silver beakers of various dates are recorded, but the demand for them lessened in the eighteenth century when glass could be obtained without difficulty and was less costly. At the end of the century there was a fashion for beakers resembling barrels, realistically engraved with staves and hoops.

BELLS

Silver bells were made throughout the eighteenth century and, in many instances formed the central feature of inkstands. However, it is likely that those of a height exceeding, say, six inches, were made and sold separately. Early examples have turned handles of solid silver, while later ones more often have them of ivory or wood.

BOXES

In addition to those included in a toilet set for use at the dressing table, silver boxes were made in many sizes and shapes for other purposes. In some instances their original purposes remain uncertain, and the names by which they are known are quite modern ones. Among the many types of boxes produced are the following:

PATCH BOXES: Usually circular and with push-on lids, which often bear engraved designs. Surviving specimens date from the seventeenth century.

SNUFF BOXES: Those who could not afford a fashionable snuff box made of gold might compromise with one of silver, pewter or papier-mâché. Silver ones varied greatly in design as well as size, and those of the early nineteenth century enjoy popularity today. Many of them have their lids cast with sporting scenes, views and so forth, which are attractive, but the present interest in them is largely due to the fact that many are suitable for holding cigarettes.

Fig. 24
Box with chased decoration, and a coat of arms on the lid. Maker's mark of Paul de Lamerie overstamping that of Paul Crespin. 1720. Width 4⅜ inches.

TOBACCO BOXES: Round or oval in shape, more often the latter, and about half an inch in depth so as to be carried easily in a pocket. The lid is loose or hinged, moulded round the rim, and often embellished with an engraved coat of arms, an elaborate monogram or an inscription.

VINAIGRETTES: Some of these are very small in size, less than an inch long. The hinged lid opens to reveal a pierced and gilt inner lid, also with a hinge, under which was kept a fragment of sponge soaked in strong perfume. The latter was sniffed to forestall an impending attack of fainting, or to ward off offensive smells and germs. Vinaigrettes were first made in the late eighteenth century and by 1800 were being turned out in large numbers, especially in Birmingham.

Fig. 25
Box embossed and chased with gad-rooning. Maker's mark F V with a coronet above, Exeter, 1705. Width 6¼ inches. Weight 17 oz. 11 dwt.

BUCKLES

Silver shoe buckles were worn during the eighteenth century, but their use was limited to those who could afford to buy them. In the late 1780's fashion decreed buckles of extra large size, and it was noted that their wearers 'were obliged to buckle them to the shoe with a false strap'. A slightly earlier report mentioned that fops wore buckles of silver weighing eight or ten ounces apiece. Presumably this was only on social occasions, as the daily round would have been made very arduous by such encumbrances.

Doubtless the majority of old silver buckles have been melted down, as once they went out of fashion they were completely useless. Examples are rare nowadays, but like buttons they appeal less to the silver collector than to specialists.

BUTTER DISHES

Silver articles designed specifically for holding butter at the table are uncommon. Among the most pleasing are those made in Ireland in the last quarter of the eighteenth century. They have pierced sides and covers and glass liners, the embossed designs being of the usual neo-classical form. To make their purpose clear a seated cow forms a convenient knob handle.

BUTTONS

Buttons were made from a very great variety of materials, including silver. In the late eighteenth and early nineteenth century the metal was used often for the buttons of Hunts and their members. The buttons are engraved or moulded in relief with the Hunt initials and insignia; thus, the Fitzwilliam shows the initials *F.H* beneath the family crests: a triple row of ostrich plumes rising from a ducal coronet and, to the right, a griffin. Likewise, the house servants of the wealthy had silver buttons on their livery, and these also bear distinctive and appropriate markings.

Less personal were sets of buttons engraved neatly with sporting subjects, which were very popular in about 1820. Many were made for the bookseller, bookbinder and print-seller Thomas Gosden, who specialised in supplying the sporting fraternity with books on their favourite subject, as well as small items to add to their pleasure.

Engraved sporting buttons include some with foxhounds, and a recorded set of ten each bears a running hound with its name. Another set shows race-horses, one of which has her jockey at her head, while above is the name of the animal *Sleeping Kate*; which can have been no invitation to punters.

Eighteenth century buttons are sometimes found with hallmarks. Being small and of slight weight they did not have to be submitted to Goldsmiths' Hall, and came under the ruling of 1738 that items weighing under 10 dwt. apiece were exempted. The introduction of duty in 1784 left the position insufficiently clear, so a new Act was passed in 1790 by which buttons, unless under 5 dwt. in weight, had to be assayed and marked.

Silver buttons are probably less the province of silver collectors than of button addicts. In England, these last are comparatively few in number. but in the United States of America the hobby has a large following, Not only are there books devoted specifically to it, but active Button Clubs publish information on the subject.

Fig. 26
Pail-shaped butter dish and cover engraved in simulation of hooped staves. Maker's mark J H, Greenock, *circa* 1800. Weight 22 oz. 14 dwt.

CADDY SPOONS

To ladle and measure the tea being taken from the caddy, a special type of spoon was made from the last quarter of the eighteenth century. The bowl is most often circular, but can in fact be of almost any shape, and although such trifles might have been of the simplest possible pattern this is only very rarely the case. Silversmiths in London, Birmingham and elsewhere exercised their ingenuity in designing and making them in a bewildering range of patterns (Plate 2).

All types of processes were employed in their making, and they can be found pierced and engraved, stamped and in filigree work, as well as embossed and chased. Copies of seashells, bunches of grapes resting on vine leaves, and jockey caps are among the many inappropriate subjects embodied in their design, and there is a lengthy list of the varieties known. Devotees to them are numerous enough to sustain the Society of Caddy Spoon Collectors, which aims 'to promote the study of a delightful memento of a gracious era.'

Many of the old patterns of caddy spoons have been reproduced in recent years and are on sale in jewellers' and silversmiths' shops. They bear the correct hallmarks and cannot disguise their lack of age. Older copies can have had their marks worn by wear, or by simulated wear,

59

until they are difficult to decipher, and an inexperienced buyer should exercise caution in purchasing examples in that condition.

CANDLESTICKS AND CANDELABRA

In the mid-seventeenth century the metal candlestick, both in silver and brass, had a large-sized central grease pan and a spreading domed foot. Within the next fifty years or so it was developed into a type that remained standard thereafter: an inverted letter T, that conformed in detail to changing fashions. First, however, the silver specimens were loth to part with the wide greasepan, and even up to about 1710 it remained visible, only a vestige of its former self and lowered down the stem to within an inch or so of the foot.

Fig. 27
Cast candlestick with octagonal base and turned stem. One of a pair by Pierre Harache, 1703. Height about 7 inches. Weight 23 oz. (pair).

The most commonly found silver candlestick of *c.* 1700 stood between six and seven inches in height, had a square or polygonal base rising to a flat disc from which sprang the main stem leading to the nozzle. The latter was fitted with a removable grease pan, often with a gadrooned rim. Similarly-decorated mouldings and vertical fluting were used elsewhere, and there was usually a small formal shield on which a crest or coat of arms could be engraved. (Plate 14).

Fig. 28
Candlesticks with shaped bases and turned and faceted stems. A set of four by Paul de Lamerie, 1744. Height 8 inches. Weight 67 oz. 11 dwt. (four).

Whereas the examples just described were built up from flat sheet silver soldered together, they were succeeded by others made from castings. The general form remained more or less unchanged for a decade or two, with a simple and satisfying appearance that has retained its attraction ever since. The octagonal base was the most popular, and this was often given

61

a faceted border and recessed centre, while the stem was eight-sided and modelled with a series of flattened spheres and inverted pear shapes closely resembling those used on contemporaneous wine-glasses. The rounded candle sockets were finished with a moulded rim and usually did not have grease pans.

Fig. 29
Candlesticks with decorated bases and stems and removable grease pans. By John Priest, 1753. Height about 9 inches. Weight 71 oz. 10 dwt. (four).

From after 1740 a change began to be noticeable and traces of the newly-introduced rococo appeared. The base became more complex in outline, with shaped corners divided by incurved sides, and the stem was enriched by having leaves and shells moulded on it. Shells sometimes appear also on the bases, and there is a partial return to the separate grease pans of 40–50 years earlier.

With changes in ornament to suit the tastes of purchasers, the candlestick did not alter appreciably until the next swing of the pendulum of fashion. The following neo-Classical style is marked in part by a liking for taller candlesticks than previously, and by the abandoning of curved lines in favour of severely straight ones. From the 6–7 inches usual at the beginning of the century, they were gradually heightened until by 1770 a full twelve inches was not uncommon.

Fig. 30
Candelabrum of rococo design. One of a pair by William Tuite, 1764. Height 20 inches. Weight 105 oz. 5 dwt. (pair).

At that date a large proportion of examples exhibit a square base with incurved sloping top, leading up to a Corinthian column or to a tapered square stem with a vase-shaped socket. Festoons of husks, oval and round discs (*paterae*) and rams' heads were embossed and chased, and fluting was executed in the form of a bat's wing: the flutes tapering and radiating.

Again there was a change in manufacturing technique, with a return to the use of thin sheet silver in place of casting. The latter resulted in the production of an article with sufficient weight to remain stable, but the taller thin metal ones were prone to be top heavy unless their bases were filled with a suitable material. Candlesticks treated in this manner are termed to be 'loaded', and are normally found to have been finished beneath the base with a piece of green baize. It not only conceals the filling, but obviates scratching of any surface on which the candlestick stands.

There was also a liking for candlesticks with their stems in the form of human figures, which had been used occasionally in the same manner at earlier dates. Harlequin was, possibly, the most popular among these rarities, but such subjects form only a small proportion of the mass of those made.

While it might have been expected that the profusion of ornament seen on so many articles during the height of the rococo style would equally have affected candlesticks, this did not occur widely. Instead, the early nineteenth century saw them being made in much more elaborate patterns than were in use 50 or 60 years before. Many of the designs current after the Regency vied with French examples of the reign of Louis XV, when the *rocaille* was at its height across the English Channel.

It will be found that up to about the middle years of the eighteenth century the majority of candlesticks were marked beneath the base: usually with one stamp in each corner, or at any rate well separated from one another. When they are present, removable grease pans frequently bear only the lion *passant* Sterling mark, and it is not uncommon to find that the pans have been added later in date so as to make the article conform to fashion.

Later in the century marks are increasingly often to be found on the side of the candle socket, after about 1775 they appear in a row along one edge of the base. However, these remarks are no more than generalisations, and there were just as many exceptions concerning the positioning of marks as there were to a particular style during its currency.

While the majority of pieces made at any one time conform to the prevailing fashion, there are always deviations from the normal. Examples made in earlier styles are not uncommon at any date, and were not always made on purpose to deceive. They may have been produced to satisfy the whim of a buyer, or to match existing articles. For the latter reason, a pair of candlesticks was quite often enlarged to a set of four or six a few years after the originals were purchased, and it is always wise to check the marks on each single component of an apparently matching set.

The design of the candelabrum, or branch candlestick, follows that of the simple candlestick, although surviving examples dating from before the mid-eighteenth century are now very scarce. At first the arms radiated outwards and upwards in gentle curves like those of a chandelier, but in time they were more intricate in pattern. Examples made from late in the century have reeded arms extending in complex scrolls to either side, and the central socket is fitted with a removable finial so that it can accommodate a candle if required. (see fig. 18, page 45).

Fig. 31
Candelabrum with a human half-figure
springing from a rococo base. One of a
pair by William Pitts, 1809, the branches
by Robert Garrard, 1829. Height about
20 inches. Weight 194 oz. (pair).

The arms are usually a separate feature which fit into the socket of the candlestick. In some instances the arms, or branch as it is termed, are by a different maker and vary in date from the candlestick. This can be because the owner of the latter subsequently added them, and they were obtained from another source.

Some makers were particularly successful with candelabra, and two names recur frequently in connexion with those of the late eighteenth century. They are John Schofield, of London (c. 1770–90), and Matthew Boulton, of Birmingham (mark entered 1773).

See also **CHAMBER CANDLESTICKS**
TAPER STICKS

CANTEENS

A pocket-sized set of knife, fork, spoon and other articles is termed a canteen. Some were in leather or shagreen cases, but others were silver throughout.

One of the most historical and neatly designed canteens was that of Prince Charles Edward, the Young Pretender, which was acquired at the Battle of Culloden in April 1746 by the victorious Duke of Cumberland. It is contained in a silver case embossed and chased with thistles and flowers and engraved with the insignia of the Prince. The set comprises two knives, two forks and two spoons of which all the handles unscrew for stowing; a spoon combined with a marrow-scoop; a container for condiments; a nutmeg grater combined with corkscrew; a quaich, and a drinking beaker.

Fig. 32/3
Bonnie Prince Charlie's canteen, found
by the Duke of Cumberland after the
battle of Culloden, 1746. By Ebenezer
Oliphant, Edinburgh, 1740. Height 6¾
inches.

Plate 9   66
(Left to right, top): saucepan and cover. Apparently no maker's mark, Edinburgh, *circa* 1790.
Weight 8 oz. 5 dwt. (all in).—Taper box and cover. By W. Tweedie, 1786. Height 2 inches. Weight
3 oz. (Bottom row): miniature tankard. Marker's mark R H, *circa* 1690. Height 1⅞ inches.—Mug
with moulded rim, base and girdle. By John Cole, 1708. Height 2½ inches. Weight 2 oz. 5 dwt.

CASTERS

By the end of the seventeenth century silver casters for powdered spices and sugar were straight-sided with a neatly spreading foot, and a pierced domed cover. The latter was surmounted by a turned finial, and was held to the body by means of a bayonet joint. The casters were often in sets of three, two small and a large one which might stand as much as nine inches in height.

In the first decades of the eighteenth century the shape changed to that of a pear (or baluster) raised on a low pedestal foot, and with rounded or faceted sides. The piercing of the tops was executed with great care and the complex designs used were in contrast to the plainness of the remainder of the article. Again, sets of three were supplied, and occasionally one of them was unpierced for use with dry mustard powder. The lids from this time onwards merely push into place, but even after more than 200 years they are found to stay in position during use.

Fig. 34
Caster engraved with a coat of arms within crossed plumes, and the lid surmounted by a cut card rosette. Maker's mark W C with a crown above and a pierced mullet (star) below, 1672. Height 5¼ inches. Weight 5 oz. 16 dwt.

By 1740 the caster had acquired an increased bulge at the base of the 'pear', and both body and cover bore decorative displays of floral and other rococo motifs. These were chased and embossed on the circumference of the body and pierced and engraved on the lid. In the third quarter of the century the pedestal grew taller, and decoration was limited to a

Plate 10   67
Pair of oval salts with gadrooned rims, shell knees and pad feet. By Robert and David Hennell (?), 1765. Width 3¾ inches. Weight 6 oz.—Mustard pot with bright cut and pierced ornament and blue glass liner. By Peter, Ann and William Bateman, 1803. Height 3⅛ inches. Weight 3 oz. 5 dwt.—Caster. By John White (?), 1762. Height 5⅛ inches. Weight 2 oz. 10 dwt.

narrow band or two of moulding and simple geometrical piercing and engraving of the lid (see Plate 10).

Fig. 35
Pear-shaped caster. By John Keigwin, 1710. Height 6⅝ inches. Weight 9 oz.

Finally, from about 1790 casters were mostly made of cut glass with small silver tops, and are found with matching bottles in frames designed to hold them. The latter had existed for most of the century, but the casters could be separated from them and were still usable. The later glass bottles being tall and slim in shape were unstable unless supported in their frames.

See **CRUET FRAMES**

68

CHAMBER CANDLESTICKS

The old nursery rhyme with the line 'Here comes a candle to light you to bed' would have referred to one in a chamber candlestick. The latter was designed and used as a portable form of indoor illumination, and was ideal for lighting the way upstairs and along dark corridors.

As they doubtless had daily usage and suffered hard wear, there are very few examples surviving from before 1700. One with the hallmark for 1688 has a circular pan and a flat handle, and others of about the same date are similar in appearance. All have been described as bearing a marked resemblance to a frying-pan.

From after 1700 chamber candlesticks begin to be less scarce, and are found to have acquired a more decorative appearance. The cast handle has become shaped and patterned, while the pan, which is sometimes raised on short feet, has a gadrooned or moulded edge.

Later, an extinguisher of matching pattern was often added, and fits by a right-angled square peg into a hole in or beside the handle. Few further refinements were possible, but some of the candlesticks of the end of the century were given an internal device for ejecting a candle stump. It was done by means of a simple plunger working within the stem of the socket, and was operated by sliding a button on the outside.

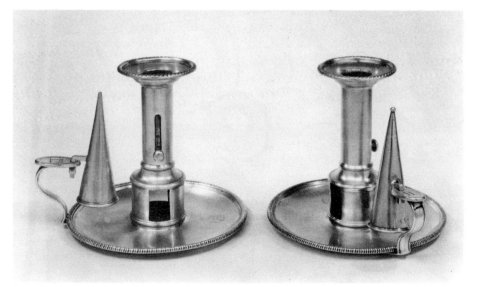

Fig. 36
Chamber candlesticks with extinguishers.
By Matthew Boulton, Birmingham, 1803.
Height 4¾ inches.

CHAMBER POTS

Silver chamber pots were made in the seventeenth century and later, but are now rare. Owners had their coats of arms, crests or initials engraved on them, and on August 29th 1715 the first Earl of Bristol noted:

> Paid Mr Chambers for a silver stew-pan weighing 67 ounces 14 dwt., & for a silver chamber pott weighing 30 ounces, both at 6s. 6d. per ounce, & for graveing them, etc., in all £32. 7. 3d.

In the days when collectors were highly selective in their buying such objects had little appeal. Unscrupulous dealers then had them converted into items that were more marketable. The easiest course taken would appear to have been to add a handle matching and opposite to the existing one, and innocently call the piece a loving-cup. As the use of the original had been completely changed it should have been re-submitted to Goldsmiths' Hall for a fresh assay, but this was not done.

CHANDELIERS

It may be imagined that chandeliers made of silver were a rarity, but they did exist and a few have survived in evidence of the fact. One at Hampton Court Palace, dates from c. 1700 and has twelve curved arms in two tiers, the central bulbous stem being surmounted by plaques bearing the Tudor rose and the fleur-de-lys. Although it is apparently undated, the maker's mark is that of George Garthorne.

Another, which was once in St. James's Palace, is now at Colonial Williamsburg, Virginia. Almost as much-travelled, but in an opposite direction, are two in the Kremlin, Moscow. They were made by Paul de Lamerie in 1734, and each has sixteen arms. A few others are in private ownership.

The largest and most sumptuous of surviving silver chandeliers is the example with seventeen branches owned by the Fishmongers' Company, and hanging in their Hall in Upper Thames Street in the City of London. Presented to the Company in 1752, an inscription on it records that it commemorates one of its members, Sir Thomas Knesworth. The maker was William Alexander, who entered his mark in 1742. The chandelier is modelled with the scrolls, leafage and other motifs current at the time, and in the centre, most appropriately, are figures of dolphins.

While other silver chandeliers are recorded in old documents, they were never plentiful. Their making and use ceased as glass ones became available, for the latter material glittered equally well in the light of candles and did not have the drawback of tarnishing.

CHEESE SCOOPS

Shovel-like cheese scoops were made from the late eighteenth century, and may be found with ivory or wood handles. Some have simple sliding devices for ejecting the soft cheese from the blade onto the plate of the diner. Others leave this little problem unsolved, and anyone who has tried to remove ripe Stilton neatly from this type of scoop will prefer the semi-mechanised variety.

CHEESE STANDS

Stands designed to hold a round of cheese, or part of one, standing on its side, were made in the eighteenth century. Mahogany examples dating from about 1770 or so are sometimes to be seen, and often perform a modern role in the guise of fruit stands. They measure about 16½ inches in width, with curved interiors and sides, and are fitted with small castors so they might be propelled about the dining table.

Silver stands would appear to have pre-dated them, as one in the Victoria and Albert Museum is hallmarked 1760. Flat-sided and with incurved ends, it has four short feet concealing castors and the sides are decoratively pierced. The design of the sides is a combination of scrolls, rosettes and trellis-pattern centred on a silhouette of the former owner's coat of arms, which is engraved. The maker was Edward Wakelin, whose firm's books are also in the Museum, and from an entry in them for the relevant year it has been learned that the piece in question was then called a 'cheese plate'.

A similar 'plate' made four years later, by which date Wakelin had acquired John Parker as a partner, was sold by Christie's in 1966. Both examples are 14¼ inches in length.

CHOCOLATE POTS

The cocoa tree was originally a native of the area about the Gulf of Mexico and down into South America, and the drink prepared from its beans was brought to Europe by the Spaniards. According to the historian, W. E. Prescott the Emperor Montezuma was extremely fond of it;

no less than 50 jars or pitchers being prepared for his own daily consumption; 2,000 more were allowed for that of his household.

The beverage reached England in the mid-seventeenth century when the following announcement was printed in the *Public Advertiser* of 16th June 1657:

In Bishopsgate St., in Queen's Head Alley, at a Frenchman's house, is an excellent West India drink, called chocolate, to be sold, where you may have it ready at any time, and also unmade at reasonable rates.

71

Fig. 37
Chocolate pot with tapering cylindrical body and hinged lids, the handle set at right angles to the spout. By Gabriel Sleath, 1711. Height 9¾ inches. Weight 27 oz. 8 dwt. (all in).

Again, according to Prescott, the Aztec Emperor had his favourite drink 'flavoured with vanilla and other spices, and so prepared as to be reduced to a froth of the consistency of honey'. Doubtless those Londoners who sampled it in Queen's Head Alley had it served in a similar form.

Once chocolate became established as a drink the silversmiths produced jugs from which it might be served. However, these cannot be distinguished from coffee pots unless they incorporate a double cover. This takes the form of an extra lid opening into the normal one, and was provided so that a rod (*molionet* or *molinet*) could be introduced to stir the mixture within. It was a refinement that prevented the escape of too much heat and steam, but possibly most people were unconcerned at this and used a pot with a normal lid.

A particularly fine example is a pot in the Victoria and Albert Museum, which has a double lid secured to the hinge by a chained pin that can be withdrawn for cleaning the vessel. The body is supported on a moulded foot and tapers upwards from an incurved base; where the handle and spout join the body are decorative reinforcements of cut card work, and the spout terminates in the head of an animal with pricked ears. It was made by William Fawdery in 1704.

Other chocolate pots made in the early years of the century are of more conventional pattern. They have straight-sided tapering bodies, but retain the moulded foot while lacking the tuck-in at the base. Some have the extra feature of a tiny hinged cover to the end of the spout, and most follow the coffee pot in having the handle placed at right-angles to the latter.

Chocolate drinking in England did not keep pace in popularity with tea and coffee, and it would seem to have had a limited appeal during the remainder of the century. Those who favoured it would have had to rely on coffee pots of silver, or alternatively made of porcelain, for few pots were apparently made specifically for chocolate after about 1710. This can be judged only by surviving examples, which in total are few, but as the drink went out of fashion it is not improbable that many of the pots once in existence were melted and re-made in other forms.

COASTERS

Coasters are circular low-rimmed stands for bottles or decanters, known in the past as bottle-stands or bottle-slides. They were first made in about 1760, and while occasionally they are completely of silver most of them have a turned wood base inset with a central silver disc for engraving with a crest or initials. Alternatively the rim is made with a shaped portion for the same purpose, in which case the disc in the base is of bone, or mother-of-pearl (Plate 8).

Typical examples are pierced with geometrical patterns and have beaded rims, while others are bright cut engraved with festoons of husks and other neo-classical ornament. Paul Storr made some exceptionally fine coasters, and a set of twelve bearing his mark and dated 1814 is in the Wellington Museum, Apsley House, London. Each of them is gilt, and the tall sides are modelled with figures of Bacchus with sleeping lions amid vine leaves and bunches of grapes. From about 1830 the rim began to be turned

73

outwards, and its upper surface was then embossed with floral and other patterns.

It is not uncommon to find the hallmarks on coasters difficult to read. In most instances they were obviously partly-obliterated during finishing when their wood bases were fitted, and dating can be estimated only from the style. They were sold usually in pairs or sets, but long sets are scarce nowadays.

See **DECANTER WAGONS**

Fig. 38
Pair of gilt coasters, the rims cast with a
pattern of vine leaves and grapes and the
interiors engraved with coats of arms.
By Benjamin Smith, 1807. Diameter 5
inches.

COFFEE POTS

John Evelyn noted in his diary that in 1637 there was at Baliol College, Oxford, 'one Nathaniel Conopios out of Greece', who drank coffee. He was perahps a lone addict, for it was several years before the habit spread. Another man who carefully noted the events of his time was Anthony à Wood, who lived in Oxford, and wrote in 1650:

This yeare Jacob a Jew opened a Coffey house at the Angel in the Parish of S. Peter in the East, Oxon., and there it was by some, who delighted in Noveltie, drunk. When he left Oxon, he sold it in Southampton buildings, in Holborn, neare London, and was living there in 1671.

The first coffee house was opened in London in 1652, when one, Mr Edwards, a Turkey merchant, brought home with him a Greek servant, whose name was Rosqua, who understood the roasting and making of coffee, till then unknown in England. This servant was the first who sold coffee; and kept a house for that purpose in George-yard, Lombard-street.

Fig. 39
Coffee pot of tapering octagonal form and with the handle set at right angles to the curved and faceted spout. By Anthony Nelme, 1720. Height 9¼ inches. Weight 28 oz. (all in).

Other reports give the name of the Greek as Pasqua Rosee, and situate his premises in St Michael's Alley, Cornhill. While a third states the owner was named Bowman, and it was his coachman who opened the business.

It seems unlikely that when served in public places the drink would have been poured from silver pots. These articles would probably not have been required until it began to be taken in the home, which did not occur until the Restoration. In 1675 Charles II ordered the closing of coffee houses because they were resorted to by those 'who devised and spread abroad divers false, malicious and scandalous reports, to the defamation of His Majesty's government, and to the disturbance of the peace and quiet of the nation.'

Fig. 40
Tapering cylindrical coffee pot with a tall domed lid and straight spout, the handle in line with the latter. By Thomas Farrer, 1727. Height 9½ inches. Weight 21 oz. 2 dwt. (all in).

The proclamation was suspended a few days after it had been announced, but no doubt it had shown that the coffee houses were officially frowned upon. If people wished to enjoy the drink (described by one writer as 'blacke as soote, and tasting not unlike it') they should do so in their own homes. The criticism had little or no effect on the prosperity of the public places; for in 1713 it was reckoned that in London alone there were 3,000 coffee houses.

The earliest recorded coffee pot is one of 1681, in the Victoria and Albert Museum. It measures $9\frac{3}{4}$ inches in height, the straight sides taper upwards from the narrow moulded base, and the hinged cover is cone-shaped with a flat button on top. The spout is straight, and is set opposite the scrolling handle. Its plain form is relieved on one side by an engraved coat of arms, and the inscription 'The Guift of Richard Sterne Esq to ye Honorable East India Compa.'

The tapering cylindrical shape of coffee pot continued to be made for the ensuing half-century, but there were a number of modifications to the simple design of the one just described. From about 1700 there was a use of cut-card work at the junctions of spout and handle, and the lid became a curved dome instead of a straight-sided cone. A few years later the spout, which had already begun to be curved, was sometimes given short ornamental scrolls at the top and base.

The rarest pots of the time are those of tapering polygonal shape, and with curved spouts similarly faceted. In a few instances the spout has the refinement of a tiny hinged cover, so that none of the aroma-laden steam might escape and lessen the strength and heat of the contents. A mark found on a number of good quality pots made in the first part of the century is that of William Fawdery, which was entered in 1698.

The feature of setting the handle at right angles to the spout appears on a proportion of the coffee pots made during the reigns of Queen Anne and George I. To many people it is the distinctive sign of an old piece, but is really comparatively rare. No doubt it is so well known because of the innumerable twentieth century reproductions of early eighteenth century pots; most of them with their handles offset, and complete with the anachronism of a matching pot for hot milk.

In the 1730s the lid was made squat in form and the spout reverted to a straight tube. Within twenty years the general shape had changed noticeably in a number of details. The spout was again curved, and was cast with a pattern where it was soldered to the body. Although the tapering outline remained, it did not continue to the foot but was 'tucked in' on the curve and raised on a low moulded base.

There followed a general conforming to the influence of rococo, and the coffee pot acquired as many shapely curves as everything else of the

77

time. The body became fully pear-shaped and the pedestal base was made taller while the spout was often cast with motifs along its whole length. The handle was composed of more than a single sweeping scroll, and became a combination of several; which must have given the carvers of wood and ivory considerable employment and taxed their skill.

At the same date, *c.* 1765, many pots were ornamented heavily with embossing and chasing, usually leaving only a small shaped space untouched for the engraving of a coat of arms. Plain examples of the period, and earlier, were the subject of attention from silversmiths active a century or so later. A noticeable proportion of surviving decorated coffee pots was embellished at a later date, when the rococo was favoured again and an unornamented surface was viewed with distaste.

By the late seventies the pot sometimes became oval in shape and vaselike in form with a tall pedestal base. The amount of embossing and chasing was lessened, and was confined to garlands of husks, fluting and beading. The overall height had risen during the course of the years, and was now an average of 12 inches, but 15-inch examples were not uncommon (Plate 12).

Alternatively, at the same date the baluster shape was revived, but with the curves given greater emphasis than before. An example of 1783 by Hester Bateman has a gadrooned foot and rim, the spout is moulded with leaves and the finial on the domed lid is in the shape of a miniature vase. Like most vessels for holding hot liquids, the handle is of carved wood, which does not conduct the heat. Occasionally makers used ivory, which was equally satisfactory for the purpose, but the employment of silver involved the introduction of insulating discs of a suitable material. This was acceptable when new, but with use the discs become mis-shapen and the pins securing the handle grow loose.

The marks on coffee pots vary in position. The majority are stamped high up and just below the neck rim, but earlier examples may be marked under the base. As with other pieces of silver there are no hard and fast rules. All separate portions, such as the lid, should have at least the lion *passant* and ideally are marked in full.

CREAM OR MILK JUGS

Small jugs for serving cream or milk, called creamers in the United States, first came into use during the reign of Queen Anne (1702–1714). As with many other vessels there was a choice of styles available at most times, and many of them appeared and re-appeared intermittently. The most popular at first was a miniature of the beer jug, but without a cover. The baluster body was raised on a short moulded foot and the handle was a simple scroll. It was a type that was much copied in China for the porcelain teasets sent here by the thousand during the ensuing years, and were duly re-copied when the English porcelain manufactories were started after 1745.

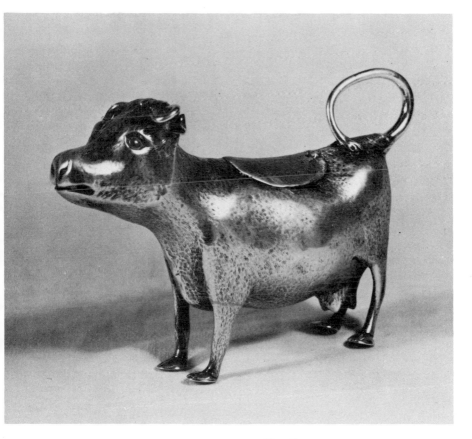

Fig. 41
Cream or milk jug in the shape of a cow, a hinged lid in the animal's back and its tail curled to form a handle. By John Schuppe, 1756. Length about 6 inches. Weight 5 oz.

At about the same time simliarly shaped jugs raised on three scrolled legs were also made, and a third variety was in the form of an inverted helmet on a short stem with a circular foot. Most of them were plain or with a band of engraving below the rim, and they averaged about 4 inches in height. Their capacity was only slight, because tea was poured from small pots into tiny cups and only a little cream would have been required.

Between about 1750 and 1760 the same shapes were in use, but were embossed and chased with scrolls, flowers and other patterns in conformity with the prevailing rococo style (Plate 4). As this became less fashionable and was replaced by the neo-classical, a change came over the appearance of cream jugs.

The Adam vase shapes were adapted, the jug became tall and thin with a handle curving up above the level of the lip and the circular base was rejected in favour of a square one. The most popular jug, judging by surviving numbers, was in the form of an elongated inverted helmet. It was generally decorated with engraved bright cut festoons with a space left for a crest or monogram. After about 1800 the helmet shape remained in favour, but was made squat and lost its pedestal so that it stood on a flat base. (Plate 4).

One unusual variety of cream jug requires a mention: that in the form of a cow. It was made with the tail curled up and over the back to form a handle, the mouth was slightly open for pouring, and a hinged lid in the centre of the back usually had a well-modelled, but out-of-scale fly as a handle. Most of them were the work of a silversmith named John Schuppe who entered his mark in 1753, and whose name indicates a Dutch origin. They have risen very steeply in value during recent years, which is remarkable considering that their appeal must surely be limited. Not only is this on account of their unpleasing (if amusing) appearance, but because they are awkward, if not well nigh impossible, to use at the table!

CRUET FRAMES

Frames for holding sets of cruets and casters at the dining table were made from early in the eighteenth century. Some were for two bottles and others held an assortment of bottles and silver casters. The former have the bottles standing in an oblong tray with handles at either end. The larger type, which is often called a 'Warwick', has a series of rings in which the containers rest, they are arranged about a central vertical handle and the whole article is raised on three short feet. After more than two centuries have elapsed it is only occasionally that one is found with both frame and contents completely matching and all bearing the same maker's mark and date letter.

Fig. 42
Cruet frame fitted with three casters and
a pair of bottles. Dublin, *circa* 1750.
Weight 53 oz. 15 dwt.

Fig. 43
Cruet frame with pierced and bright cut
decoration. By Henry Chawner, 1794.
Width 7 inches.

Plate 11   **82**
Two pairs of sugar tongs. By Hester Bateman, *circa* 1785. Length 5¼ inches. Weight of each 1 oz.—
Sugar nips. By W. Hunter (?), *circa* 1750. Length 4⅝ inches. Weight 1 oz. 5 dwt.—Apple corer (see
Plate 6). By J. Willmore, Birmingham, 1819. Length open 4¼ inches, closed 2½ inches. Weight 10
dwt.—Knife and three-pronged fork. By S. Pemberton, Birmingham, 1813. Length of knife 7 inches.

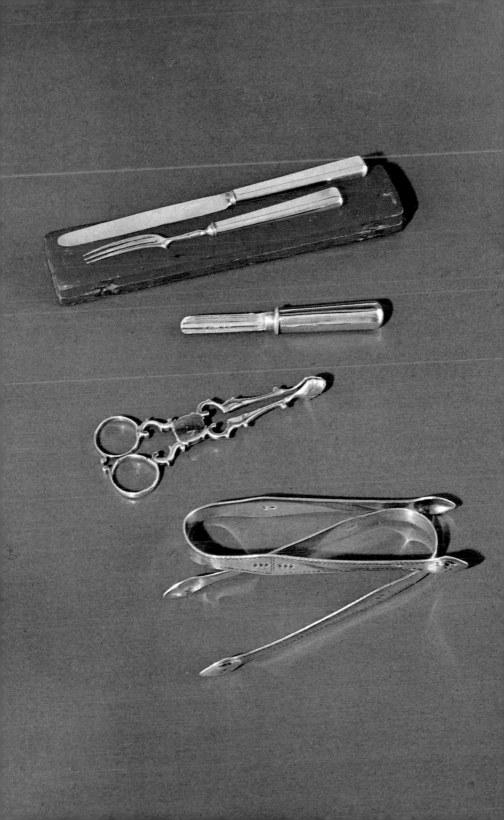

Towards the end of the century the frames were made oval, boat-shaped or oblong, and fitted throughout with silver-mounted cut-glass bottles. The sides of the frames were usually pierced and engraved with bright cut ornament, and the bases made from mahogany. Having lost their complement of bottles they have sometimes been given a further lease of life by removing the handle and filling the hole through which it is held by a nut. The remaining portion then becomes a deep-sided and useful, even if slightly odd-looking, 'tidy' or sweetmeat container.

Early in the nineteenth century the open Warwick returned to favour, but its appearance unmistakably reveals its age because of its squat form as well as by the motifs decorating it. A glance at the marks will quickly settle any doubts.

See **CASTERS**
WINE AND SAUCE LABELS

DECANTER WAGONS

Pairs of coasters were sometimes made linked together and mounted on wheels or castors, so that they could be moved easily on the dining-table. An exceptional example sold at Sotheby's was in the form of a ship's Jolly-boat.

Decanter wagons are an excellent aid to keeping the Port moving, but meet with disaster if guiding hands are unsteady.

See **COASTERS**

DINNER SERVICES

Services of silver which included everything necessary for the dinner table were made with matching pieces during the eighteenth century. A typical example is one that belonged to Sir John Cust, and was sold at Christie's in 1963. It was supplied by the Royal Jewel Office when Sir John was elected Speaker of the House of Commons, each item being engraved with the Royal arms and with his own. When he was re-elected to the office in 1768 he had a further issue of plate, and he died in 1770 five days after having resigned from Parliament.

The service, of simple pattern with gadrooning on the rims, comprised:

48 dinner plates	836 oz.	0 dwt.
12 soup plates	216 oz.	0 dwt.
12 dishes, 12 to 20¼ ins.	444 oz.	0 dwt.
4 second-course dishes	83 oz.	10 dwt.
4 entrée dishes	76 oz.	15 dwt.

Plate 12   83
Coffee pot of baluster form with beaded mouldings. Maker's mark worn, 1784. Height 12¼ inches. Weight 27 oz. 5 dwt. (all in).

a mazarine	38 oz. 17 dwt.
a tureen and cover	103 oz. 16 dwt.
4 sauce tureens with stands and ladles	121 oz. 2 dwt.
8 table candlesticks	200 oz. (approx.)

The total weight comes to 2,123 oz. 8 dwt.

See **DISHES**
　　MAZARINES
　　SAUCE BOATS
　　TUREENS

DISH CROSSES

The dish cross is an X-shaped support for a dish, hinged centrally and adjustable to a required diameter by means of sliding supports. Not only does it hold dishes of many sizes, but their contents can be kept warm with the spirit-lamp forming part of the device. They are useful adjuncts to the dining table, and eighteenth century silversmiths also made them

Fig. 44
Dish cross adjustable to hold a dish of
any diameter up to about 15 inches.
By Burrage Davenport, 1774.

84

decorative by shaping and piercing the supports. Most examples date from the last quarter of the eighteenth century, and occasionally Irish ones some 40–50 years earlier can be found.

DISHES

From about the middle of the eighteenth century a selection of dishes for different purposes was available. They varied in size and shape, and while the decoration on them took a number of forms it was usually quite simple and confined to ornamental mouldings like the reed-and-tie. They included the following:

Entree dishes: covered dishes, often with a removable ring handle so that the cover could be reversed and used as a dish. It is not uncommon to find examples made after 1800 with silver or plated stands enclosing spirit burners.

Meat dishes: oval in shape and ranging in width from about 10 to 30 inches.

Second-course dishes: circular, and from 10 to 16 inches in diameter.

Venison dishes: large-sized meat dishes, but with channels leading to a well in which gravy can collect.

After the turn of the century the same types of dishes continued to be made, but were usually more heavily decorated.

DISH RINGS

These circular stands, because of the fact that many were made in Ireland in the eighteenth century and because the Irish like potatoes, have often been called 'Potato Rings'. They were first made in England at the beginning of the eighteenth century, but the majority of Irish examples are dated *c.* 1770. They were supposedly used to support a bowl of steaming potatoes, which they probably did, but equally they carried a bowl of hot punch. In both instances they prevented the heat from damaging a polished table surface. They performed this insulation most efficiently because of the piercing in their sides, which is usually considered to be only a decorative feature.

Dish rings were not only pierced, but their patterns were embossed and chased and gave considerable scope for inventiveness on the part of the maker. Late eighteenth century examples are patterned formally with, for instance, draped ribbons or husks against a geometrical or leafy background. Those of about 1770 show rustic scenes with milkmaids and even pigsties and pigs, or more sophisticated buildings and their inhabitants. In each instance the ornament is in the form of a vignette set in elaborate rococo scrolls, flowers and acanthus leaves.

Period examples of the rings are quite uncommon, but they have been extensively copied for many years. Such modern ones are, of course, correctly hallmarked, and there should be no difficulty in distinguishing old from new.

DOG COLLARS

Owners of pets gave them silver collars to wear, although it remains unrecorded whether the animals were flattered. Very few of the collars have survived, as the softness of silver when compared with, say, brass made the precious metal impractical for the purpose.

The account-books of Sir Richard Myddelton, of Chirk Castle, Denbighshire, contain an entry for 24th March, 1707, noting the purchase of:

A silver coller for Mr Wm Myddelton's little dog . . . 10s.

Undoubtedly only a collar of silver would have been worthy of having engraved on it the lines written by Alexander Pope on the occasion of his making a gift to Frederick, Prince of Wales, son of George II. The lines were on the collar of a dog which the poet sent to the Prince, who lived at Kew Palace, and were:

I am his Highness' dog at Kew;
Pray tell me, sir, whose dog are you?

The eighteenth century collars were adjustable in diameter, fitted with a hasp so they could be padlocked in place, and varied in width and diameter according to the breed of dog for which they were intended. An inner lining of thin leather provided for the comfort of the wearer.

DRINKING-CUPS

Tall-stemmed drinking cups, resembling wine-glasses, date back to the sixteenth century. Examples of that time are very rare, but a number have been preserved from most decades of the seventeenth century, and they enable changes in style to be followed. After George Ravenscroft had introduced his newly-devised glass-of-lead between 1674 and 1676 quantities of it began to reach the market in place of imported supplies. Its novelty and attractiveness diminished the demand for silver drinking-vessels, and the latter would seem to have been seldom made at that time.

Towards the end of the eighteenth century they were revived. The bowls are found variously ornamented with embossing, chasing and engraving, but it is doubtful if they were intended for actual use. The large majority of surviving examples bear inscriptions showing that their principal purpose to have been for presentation as trophies.

86

EGG CUPS

Egg cups, like so many other articles for use at the table, were made of silver from the end of the eighteenth century. Often they were supplied in pairs or sets, which were mounted in a frame provided with places for spoons and salt.

Egg boilers have also survived from about the same period. They comprise a framework holding a spirit lamp, above which is a water container in which the eggs could be placed and boiled as required. To bring peace of mind to devotees of the three-minute egg (or, for that matter, to those preferring the four-minute variety) the cover is fitted with a small sandglass.

It may be wondered what kind of article was referred to by Isabella Hervey, wife of the future first Earl of Bristol, who noted in her husband's expenses book on 3rd February 1690:

Daer cousen donn gave me a silver egg thing worth ten ginnes.

Whatever the 'egg thing' may have been it vanished long ago, and only the written record of its existence remains.

EPERGNES

The épergne is a decorative centrepiece for the dining table, introduced early in the eighteenth century. It was devised to hold pickles, sweetmeats and other delicacies conveniently in the middle of the table so that they could be reached by all the diners. It takes the form of a framework with suitable provision for supporting dishes and suspending baskets, while some have also arms and sockets for candles.

Early examples of the épergne tend to be heavy in both weight and appearance, but by the mid-century they had lightened in both senses. Their makers included Thomas Powell, who entered his mark in 1758 and would appear to have made little else. He incorporated in his work all the varied ornament available during the height of the rococo style, combining French, Chinese and Gothic motifs to great effect.

Rivalling the adaptability of his contemporary, Thomas Chippendale the cabinet-maker, Powell was equally at home in making épergnes in the neo-classical style. One of his, hallmarked 1778, in the Victoria and Albert Museum, has curved arms holding eight baskets or bowls of two sizes in two tiers, and a central support rising to a large-sized bowl. All the containers are pierced and decorated with festoons of laurel leaves, as well as having oval medallions for the owner's crest.

The following century saw the introduction of bigger and heavier pieces than before. They were often no more than metal sculptures with projecting candle-arms; a combination of the épergne and the candelabra with more bulk than beauty (see fig. 11, page 29).

Fig. 45
Epergne cast with a pattern of flowers and leaves and fitted with removable pierced baskets. By Thomas Powell, 1770. Height 20 inches.

EWERS AND BASINS

Prior to the general use of forks, food was cut up and conveyed to the mouth with the aid of a knife and the assistance of the diner's fingers. Three or four guests would often share a single dish, and out of respect for each other the least they could do was to clean their fingers from time to time during the meal. To this end, the table of the wealthy host was equipped with a silver ewer filled with perfumed water, and a basin into which it was poured for use.

Sixteenth and seventeenth century examples are so rare that they are most unlikely to come within the province of many collectors. While the articles vary in form, all were the subject of elaborate ornamentation and many of them were gilt. The ewer is raised on a tall foot, usually circular, and the basin, which is round or oval, is often little deeper than a soup plate.

A gilt vase-shaped ewer and circular basin of 1592 are both chased all over with a complex pattern of strapwork and leaves, while the centre of the basin rises to a boss. Another, of 1638 and of plain silver, comprises a tall-footed ewer of inverted helmet shape, and a basin recessed in the form of five petals. The latter, as that of earlier date, has a central boss, and both pieces bear a coat of arms.

Forks had become customary by the end of the seventeenth century, and the ewer and basin were no longer essential at the table. In spite of this, they continued to be made and took their place as display pieces on dining room sideboards. The most sumptuous of them is the ewer and basin made of solid gold, at Chatsworth, Derbyshire, which is illustrated in the fronts-piece to J. F. Hayward's *Huguenot Silver in' England*, (1959). It was the work of a French-born silversmith, Pierre Platel, in 1701, and remains in the possession of the descendants of the nobleman for whom it was made, the Duke of Devonshire.

The Chatsworth ewer is helmet-shaped with lobes in relief on the lower part of the body, a shaped moulded band centred on an ornament above the engraved coat of arms, and a moulded rim. The foot is circular with a gadrooned edge and panels of scale engraving, while the finely designed flying handle is in the form of a caryatid. The basin, which is equally accurately described as a deep dish, is oval, with a shaped border modelled with scrolls and shells and with an engraved coat of arms in the centre.

Later pieces, made by de Lamerie and others, were also helmet-shaped, of striking appearance and incorporate rococo elements in their ornament. By the mid-century they started to go out of fashion and few were made after then.

After 1700 their purpose was solely ostentation: to indicate their owner's financial standing in a manner habitual at the time. Be that as it may, the ewers in particular were the object of considerable thought and skill on the part of designers and craftsmen, and some of the surviving specimens can be numbered among the finest expressions of their art.

EXTINGUISHERS

Extinguishers are small conical caps (in appearance exactly like old-fashioned dunce's caps) for placing on top of a candle to extinguish it. They are usually found fitted into the handle of a chamber candlestick, where they are readily available when needed. Usually each extinguisher has a short square right-angled peg soldered halfway down the side, and this fits into a square hole made to receive it.

Another and rarer variety of extinguisher is similar to a pair of sugar nippers, with a scissor-like action. The end grips are not hollowed, but completely flat so as to squeeze the wick and put out the flame. They are known as Douters.

FISH SLICES

The fish slice is so similar in appearance to the cake slice that unless some piscatory emblem is visible they cannot be told apart. However, silver-smiths often decorated the blades appropriately with fishes of various kinds, and in such instances there can be no doubt. The cake, on the other hand, does not lend itself so readily to the same end, and plain-bladed slices or servers were possibly for use at the tea table.

The Ashmolean Museum, Oxford, possesses a fish slice made by Paul de Lamerie in 1741, but the majority of surviving examples are of later date. The de Lamerie one has an oval-shaped blade, pierced and engraved with rococo scrolls, shells and fishes and is as well-finished as the more important works of the master.

Late eighteenth century fish slices vary in outline between the pointed oval and a triangle with curved sides and, occasionally, take the form of a fish of scarcely recognisable species. All show careful design and workman-ship in combining neo-classical motifs with marine forms. Both plain and bright cut engraving were employed to give detail to the silhouetted shapes (Plate 11).

The slices were given handles no less varied in pattern than the blades, and while some were of silver others were of green-stained ivory. The silver-smiths who made them include the industrious Hester Bateman, and it is not uncommon to find that the handle came from a different workshop from the blade and accordingly bears the mark of another maker. This does not necessarily mean that the two parts have been united in modern times, but suggests strongly that handle-making was a specialised branch of silversmithing.

Nineteenth century fish slices were usually of irregular shape, with an upcurved pointed end. Their decoration was little different from that employed earlier, but was seldom as delicate in pattern and rarely as well executed. In due time the slice was paired with a matching fork and both were given plain polished ivory handles. They were sold in a leather-covered case with a shaped velvet-lined interior.

FORKS

Forks were known from early times, but their general use at the table does not seem to have begun until the Restoration. Queen Elizabeth possessed a number of them, but their presence in her inventory has been explained by stating that they were for serving or eating fruit. Alternatively, that they were presents to her from foreign visitors, in whose native lands they were commonplace.

That England was a stranger to them is made clear in a well known passage written by Thomas Coryate, who was travelling in various countries in 1608. Three years later he published *Coryats Crudities*, in which he recorded his impressions, which included:

I observed a custom in all those Italian cities and towns through which I passed that is not used in any other country that I saw in my travels, neither do I think that any other nation of Christendom doth use it, but only Italy. The Italian, and also most strangers that are commorant in Italy, do always at their meals use a little fork when they cut their meat . . . their forks being for the most part of iron or steel, and some of silver, but those are used only by gentlemen. . . Hereupon I myself thought to imitate the Italian fashion by this fork cutting of meat, not only when I was in Italy, but also in Germany, and often-times in England since I came home.

There are other references of about the same date arguing for and against importing the outlandish habit into England. However, although it may have been adopted by the few, there seems little doubt that its employment remained limited until the second half of the century. This receives confirmation from the fact that only a single fork has survived from the years before 1650. It is an example in the Victoria and Albert Museum, two-pronged with a long flat square-ended handle, hallmarked 1632 and engraved with the crests of the former noble owner and his wife.

While the fork began to be used more generally after Charles II ascended the throne, it was many years before it became a normal feature of the table. Survivors of late seventeenth date are sufficiently few to indicate that they were never plentiful. The earliest existing set comprises nine forks hallmarked 1667, each with three prongs and trefid (or trifid) terminals which came from the Elizabethan mansion on Plymouth Sound, Mount Edgcumbe, and bear the crest of the Edgcumbe family. A slightly later set, sold by auction at Sotheby's in 1969 consisted of six two-pronged examples, also with trefid terminals, of which two were hallmarked 1694 and four a year later.

A similar variation in the number of prongs occurred throughout the eighteenth century, and would have been a matter of choice on the part of the buyer. Four prongs gradually came into use in the years after 1750, but the other types continued to be made in the provinces. Handles of forks matched those of spoons.

At one time it was a profitable deceit for a dishonest craftsman to convert a useless damaged spoon, complete with a good set of marks, into a much more desirable and rare fork. With this fact in mind, a collector should examine specimens with care or buy only from a trustworthy source.

HONEY JARS

In the past, honey was served at the table, but little is known about any vessels that may have been designed especially to contain it until the end of the eighteenth century. In the early 1790s Paul Storr made a jar in the shape of a straw hive, or skep, after the original that was made from bundles of straw bound with strips of rose branch to form a dome. It was reproduced carefully by means of casting and engraving, and realism went so far as to make the handle, in some cases, a model of a bee.

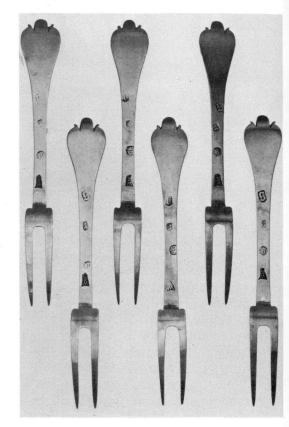

Fig. 46
Six forks with trefid terminals. By William Scarlett, two 1694 and four 1695. Weight about 4 oz.

Storr's pots are completed by a recessed dish, some $5\frac{1}{2}$ inches in diameter, which has a border simulating bound straw to match the skep. Of recorded examples of these attractive articles, some are gilt, and one hallmarked 1798 has the stand engraved with the Royal crown and cypher of Queen Charlotte, wife of George III.

Fig. 47
One of a pair of gilt ice pails ornamented with bands of vine leaves and grapes and with applied cast coats of arms, the handles springing from bearded Assyrian masks. By Benjamin Smith, 1807. Height 12¾ inches, width of stands 10¾ inches. Weight 284 oz. (pair).

ICE PAILS

Silver vessels to hold ice for cooling a single bottle of wine at the table were made from the end of the seventeenth century, and are known either as ice pails or wine coolers. A few of these early examples have survived, including one of 1698 belonging to the Duke of Devonshire and a pair at Ickworth, Suffolk, which were owned formerly by the Earls of Bristol and are now in the care of the National Trust. The latter, made by a prominent Huguenot silversmith, Philip Rollos, who enjoyed the patronage of both William III and George I, although without date-letters can be attributed by their style and from the armorial bearings engraved on them to the years between 1715 and 1720.

The general use of the ice pail did not occur until towards the end of the eighteenth century, when the large-sized wine cistern finally became obsolete. From about 1780 pails formed part of the dinner service and were made in styles matching the tureens and sauce containers, and are found in pairs or multiples of two up to a total of a dozen.

The shape of the pail is usually simple, either straight-sided or with a curved base raised on a low pedestal foot. While ornament in the years 1780–1800 was often slight, after the turn of the century makers like Paul Storr and Benjamin Smith introduced elaborate decorative features. The former made a number in the shape of the celebrated Warwick Vase; a classical marble vase found in an Italian lake in 1770, which was brought to England and sold to the Earl of Warwick four years later. As it is ornamented with masks and emblems of Bacchus it made an appropriate model for a wine bottle holder.

The pails were made with a removable inner liner and rim, so that the ice was kept separate from the bottle. The latter was chilled but did not get wet, and when removed did not leave a trail of drips.

INKSTANDS

The inkstand, or standish, was known in Tudor times, but the earliest surviving English example is dated 1630. As with so many other silver articles it is rare to find anything that was made prior to the Restoration, and much of our information of what preceded that event is owed to inventories and other documents.

The most enduring form is the so-called 'Treasury' type, which is a flat oblong box divided lengthways. It has two lids folding from a central long hinge where there is also a carrying handle, and the whole is raised on short feet. In one side are usually fitted an inkpot and a container for pounce, while the other holds pens.

No doubt they acquired their name because it was the accepted pattern for ministerial use. In 1932 E. Alfred Jones noted that there were three of them hallmarked 1685 in the Treasury, while the offices of the Privy Council contained eight: four of which were made in 1685 and four in 1702. They continued to be in demand throughout the eighteenth and nineteenth centuries, and are no doubt still being made, for they are both satisfactory in appearance and convenient in use.

The mention of a pounce container may require some explanation, and this item, which usually matches the inkpot, is sometimes referred to more correctly as a sand box. Pounce is a name for pumice, an abrasive powder used to smooth parchment preparatory to writing on it. It was replaced by fine sand for drying the ink following the employment of paper for letter-writing, and sand remained in use even after blotting paper was obtainable.

Soon after 1700 an alternative pattern of inkstand began to be made. It is a rectangular tray on low feet, fitted with an inkpot, a pounce or sand box, and a bell or a taper stick; the latter being placed in the centre. There were innumerable variations of detail, such as the shaping of the tray, the mouldings on its rim and on the fittings, and the design of the feet.

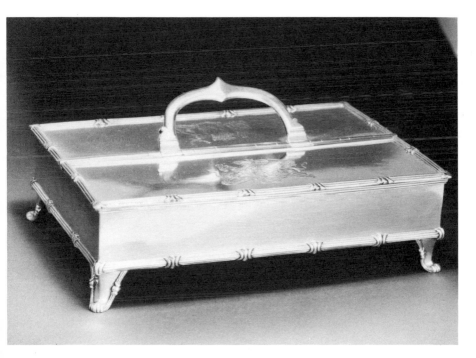

Fig. 48
Inkstand of 'Treasury' type. Maker's mark H N, 1805. Length 12 inches.

95

Fig. 49
Inkstand, the deep tray fitted with three
pots for ink, pounce and pens, all
engraved with the Royal arms and cypher
of George I. By Philip Rollos, 1716.
Width 12¾ inches. Weight 65 oz. 9 dwt.

Often the top of the inkpot was drilled with holes around the perimeter,
and in these the quill pens stood. Otherwise a drawer would be provided,
or an open pot for lead shot, which not only held the pens upright but
cleaned away any ink with which they might have become encrusted.

In the second half of the eighteenth century, the trays were often bordered
by a gallery, an inch or so in height, pierced with a pattern matching that
on smaller galleries holding the fittings in place. These were then being
made of glass, decorated with cutting and topped by silver lids. Sometimes
a shaped recess was made in the tray in which the pens were laid.

A type of inkstand which enjoyed a vogue in the years about 1800 takes
the form of a globe mounted on a stem and circuar foot. The upper half of
the sphere is divided into segments which fall away to disclose the fittings
within. An example sold at Sotheby's in 1969 stood 6 inches high, was made
by John Robins in 1800, and had the unusual feature of a perpetual
calendar engraved on the foot.

Fig. 50
Inkstand of rococo design. By John
Edwards, 1744. Width 16½ inches. Weight
114 oz.

JUGS

Large-sized jugs, singly or in pairs, with and without hinged covers, were
used from the early years of the eighteenth century, but their exact purpose
must remain uncertain. At various times and by various people they have
been termed beer jugs, claret jugs, wine jugs and shaving jugs, but as almost
all of them resemble one another it is usually a question of giving them a
name likely to make them saleable.

The majority of the jugs have pear-shaped bodies, short pouring lips and
scrolled handles. Many are completely plain, but mid-century examples
were often given elaborate decoration. A pair of this nature, sold by
Sotheby's in 1969, was particularly outstanding. They were made by Phillips
Garden, who is known to have bought Paul de Lamerie's patterns and tools
when they were sold by auction after the latter's death in 1751. Made in
1754, standing 13½ inches in height and weighing no less than 175 oz.
12 dwt. they were catalogued as follows:

Fig. 51
One of a pair of jugs of rococo design. By
Phillips Garden, 1754. Height 13½ inches.
Weight 175 oz. 12 dwt. (pair).

A pair of George II baluster covered beer jugs of exceptional quality. The bodies each engraved on one side with contemporary armorials and on the other with crests within applied *rocaille* cartouches above further decoration incorporating pairs of *putti* grouped about barrels amid chased barley and hop-bine motifs, with similarly chased decorated short lidded spouts rising from female masks, finely chased multi-scroll handles, and hinged covers applied with further scrolling hop-bine finials enriched at random intervals with well modelled insects and lizards.

Fig. 52
Two jugs with partly-fluted bodies and lids. (Left) by Thomas Folkingham, 1715, and (right) by Francis Singleton, 1702. Height 11¼ inches. Weight 71 oz. (two).

From the appearance on these jugs of barley and hops it is likely that they were originally intended to hold beer. Even plain water might taste like nectar when poured from such magnificent vessels.

99

At the end of the eighteenth century jugs of similar type formed part of the tea service, and would have taken the place of a kettle or a tea urn. Some of the sets made by Paul Storr and his contemporaries have the jug raised on a stand and with a spirit lamp, and in this case the sole difference is that the kettle has a spout, whereas the jug has a lip.

See **CREAM OR MILK JUGS**

Fig. 53
Pair of jugs with leaf-capped scroll handles. By Edward Wakelin, 1754. Height 9½ inches. Weight 84 oz. 18 dwt. (pair).

KETTLES AND URNS

During most of the eighteenth century the teapot was of noticeably small size. No doubt this was originally dictated by the high cost of tea, but the habit continued for fully a half-century after the price of the leaf had become more reasonable. The small pot required frequent re-filling, and a silver one was normally accompanied at the table by a kettle. It was supplied complete with a stand containing a heater, and there was often an accompanying tray, sometimes triangular in shape, to prevent heat and drips reaching the table top.

Fig. 54
Kettle with stand and tray. By Paul de
Lamerie, 1741. Diameter of tray 11¼
inches. Weight 96 oz. (all in).

Early examples, dating to just before 1730 were equipped with an enclosed stand which held a charcoal burner, but this was soon replaced by an open frame with a spirit lamp. The kettle itself was of a flattened spherical shape with a swing handle over the top, the scrolled spout being often the sole decorative feature. In many instances the base of the kettle fitted inside a ring round the top of the stand, and it was held in place at front and rear by chained pins. They formed hinges, so that if the rear pin was withdrawn it was easy to tip and pour from the kettle without having to lift it up. With both pins in place the whole article could safely be carried about without the certainty of disaster.

While many kettles were almost devoid of ornamentation, except for a band of engraving and a coat of arms, some were of elaborate design. Typical of them is an example by Charles Kandler in the Victoria and Albert Museum. It was made between 1727 and 1737 and is embossed and chased with figures of Neptune and Amphitrite in a sea-chariot with attendant cupids. The spout is ingeniously designed as a man blowing a conch shell, the sides of the hinged handle are mermaids, and the supports of the stand take the form of mermen. It has a triangular tray bordered with shell and other ornament, and is raised on lions'-paw feet.

Some of the kettles were given stands that reached down to the floor. They resemble the highly popular tripod-based mahogany tables that generally have carved 'pie-crust' edged tops, but the kettle stand rose to a circular frame holding a spirit lamp. A few of them have survived the ever-hungry melting-pot, and one of them is in the Victoria and Albert Museum. It dates from about 1725 but is completely without marks, and is 27½ inches high.

Soon after the middle of the eighteenth century the kettle was supplanted by the tea urn. It has no separate stand, but is raised from the table by four small feet, and in place of a spout has a tap at the front of the body. Heating of the water was by means of an iron bar, which was made hot in the fire and then put into a cavity provided for it inside the vessel.

The earlier urns, dating from about 1760, were of pear shape (Plate 1), but later they were made in neo-classical vase forms and decorated with bright cut engraving.

KNIVES

Silver-handled steel knives are rare prior to about 1700, and have tapering round or polygonal handles. The most popular shape for them, the pistol, came later and remained continually in production for many decades. Towards the end of the eighteenth century many of the handles were of stamped silver sheet, soldered along the lengthways join and filled with resin.

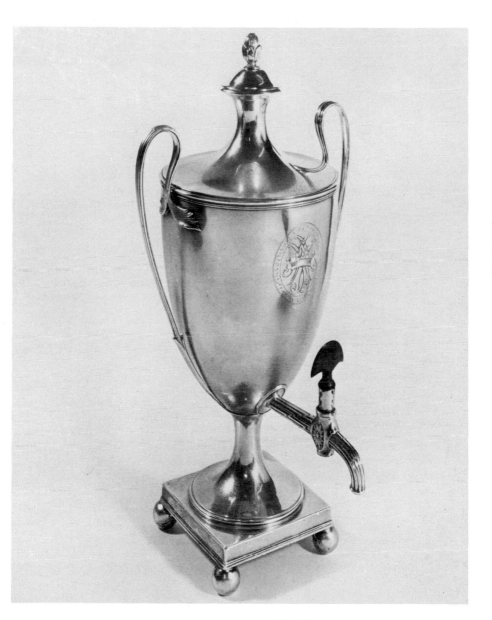

Fig. 55
Urn of neo-classical vase form, the spout
reeded and the side of the tap ornamented
with a patera. By Abraham Peterson and
Peter Podie, 1785.

103

Dessert knives, with matching spoons and forks, were gilt to prevent them becoming tarnished from contact with fruit acids. They were of smaller size than table knives and are rare before about 1800. Later still in date are fish eaters, matching knives and forks, which often have silver blades and ivory handles.

LADLES

Ladles were made in many sizes and for many purposes, and while some are quite plain others have both handle and bowl ornamented with embossed or engraved decoration. They all have in common a curved handle to which is attached, more or less at right-angles, a circular or oval bowl.

The largest ladles were those for serving soup from a tureen, and the smallest were for use in mustard pots and salt cellars. In between were others for sauce boats, and there were small-sized ones with pierced bowls for sugar. The latter, sugar-sifters, were often prettily decorated with engraving and had the holes arranged in an attractive pattern. (Plate 2).

See **PUNCH LADLES**

MARROW SCOOPS

Eighteenth century diners enjoyed eating the marrow to be found in the cavities of bones, but the delicacy was not easily accessible. To remove it, the silversmiths made scoops designed with a wide channel at one end and a narrow one at the other. Alternatively they provided a spoon of which the handle was formed as a scoop. The popularity of marrow-eating can be gauged by the large number of surviving scoops, which nowadays find a use for serving pickles and other eatables more to twentieth century taste (Plate 3).

Marrow scoops bear the usual hallmarks, but these are very often illegible. The marking was done halfway or so through manufacture, and became semi-obliterated when the article was being finished.

MAZARINES

A mazarine is an oval pierced plate which fits into a dish and is used in the serving of fish. According to Dr Norman Penzer it acquired its name from a mazer, meaning a deep dish, and is not, as might be supposed, connected with the famous Cardinal Mazarin. It was made from the early years of the eighteenth century, but examples of any date are not plentiful. Each has a narrow rim to rest on the border of the accompanying dish and the principal surface of the mazarine is slightly sunken.

The pattern of the piercing offered scope to the designer and there was a considerable variation in those made. Almost all of them included a space for engraving a coat of arms, which occupied a central position. The most attractive of them is probably a pair of silver-gilt examples in the possession of Her Majesty the Queen. They are hallmarked 1762, were made by George Hunter, and each is cut out and engraved with a representation of a net filled with many kinds of fish.

MINIATURES

Miniature copies of everyday wares were made of silver from the late seventeenth century onwards. A wide range was covered and included such diverse objects as candlesticks, tankards, kettles, teapots, coffee pots, dishes and trays. They were copied carefully from full-size examples of the period, but only a proportion bear marks enabling them to be dated. Many of them have no more than a maker's mark as they were so small as to have space for only a single stamp and they were too light in weight to require more by law.

Fig. 56
Miniature pieces; (left to right—back row) porringer by J. Beale, 1719; another, gilt, by the same, 1695; another by the same, 1706. (Front row) four-piece set by D. Clayton, *circa* 1730. Average height one inch.

105

At one time they were described as travellers' samples, but it is now generally believed they were intended as novelties. In the nineteenth century many thousands of small objects of a similar description were imported from Holland and elsewhere, and in the present century tiny reproductions of Georgian pieces have been made in England. The former bear a variety of marks, and the latter should give clear indications of their origin.

MONTEITHS

These bowls owe their name to a man who caught the public imagination while he was alive, but of whom nothing is known other than the brief facts given by Anthony Wood (or á Wood). The latter lived at Oxford where he spent many years preparing his *History and Antiquities of the University* and other works, as well as keeping copious notes of contemporary people and events. Of the monteith he wrote in 1683:

> This yeare in the summer time came up a vessel or bason notched at the rim to let drinking glasses hang there by the foot so that the body or drinking place might hang in the water to cool them. Such a bason was called a 'Monteigh' from a fantastical Scot called 'Monsieur Monteigh', who, at that time or a little before, wore the bottome of his cloake or coate so notched: U U U U.

The monteith resembled a punch bowl, but with a shaped rim instead of a level one. It must have been found both inconvenient and expensive to have two large-sized vessels for use on each occasion, so within a few years they were combined. This was done in a simple manner by making the rim removable; so the glasses were cooled, then the water was emptied and replaced by the beverage.

Fig. 57
Monteith of plain pattern, the bowl divided by chased lines and engraved with a coat of arms within a mantling of crossed plumes. By George Garthorne, 1684. Diameter 12⅝ inches. Weight 48 oz.

On the whole, the monteith received more attention from silversmiths than did the punch bowl. Ornament varied between vertical fluting and panels divided by scrolls or simple ribs, in many cases with the semi-spherical body raised on a moulded foot with a band of gadrooning. The skill of designers and craftsmen was concentrated on the rim and on the pair of ring handles at either side. The shaped rim, removable or fixed, was normally composed of scrolls broken by female or cherub heads and husk-like motifs, with the handles swinging from the mouths of lion-masks.

The monteith enjoyed popularity between about 1685 and 1720, although punch-drinking continued well beyond that time.

MUGS

A small-sized tankard which was made without a lid is usually termed a mug. At the end of the seventeenth century a very popular type had a spherical body with a reeded neck and a scrolled handle. Silver examples in this shape are not common, but it was much used at the time as a model for examples in stoneware and porcelain; the latter from China.

Fig. 58
Mug with scroll handle. By W. Andrews, 1697. Height 2¼ inches. Weight 2 oz. 5 dwt.

Eighteenth century mugs follow the succession of styles seen in tankards. They began with straight sides, then came the baluster type and finally the barrel shape.

MUSTARD POTS

Mustard acquired its name from the French, *moutarde*, which in turn came from the Latin word for unfermented wine: *mustum*. The latter was mixed with the powdered seed of the plant when it was used as a seasoning, as it is now. In England, however, the powder is more usually combined with water.

At one time, like most other substances, the·mustard seeds were pounded by the housewife with the aid of a pestle and mortar. In the early eighteenth century a Mrs Clements of Durham is said to have been the first person to have ground mustard in a mill, and sell the bright yellow powder ready for use. 'Durham Mustard' received the approval of Royalty, and thenceforward the condiment was an important feature of mealtimes.

Whether prepared painstakingly in the kitchen or bought in the ready-ground form, mustard appeared at the table for a considerable period in its dry state. It was put into tall containers which resembled casters, and in fact usually formed one of a set with them, but which had the covers unpierced, or had the piercing made 'blind' or useless by means of an inner sleeve (see **CASTERS**).

The change from dry to wet mustard took place in the middle years of the century. The familiar squat pot had appeared earlier than that, two have been noted with hall marks for 1724, but they were made before the fashion became widespread. Both forms of the seasoning continued to be popular for some years, and Worcester porcelain caster-shaped lidded pots for the dry variety are recorded which date from *c.*1755–60. At the same time the factory was also making low-sided circular pots with covers and spoons.

The silversmith did what he could to vary the shapes and decoration of wet mustard pots once they had settled into general favour. They appear as circular, oval or octagonal vessels with hinged tops and curled handles. The lids usually have a thumbpiece like that of a tankard, and this offered some slight scope for varied decorative treatment. The most popular ornament was piercing, with or without engraving, and the pot was therefore fitted with a blue glass liner (see Plate 10).

NUTMEG GRATERS

The nutmeg is the kernel of the fruit of a tree native to the East Indies. The kernels vary in shape according to the sex of the tree, those of the male being spherical, but it is said that the female are preferred because they are more aromatic; a fact conducive to speculation. The principal use of the nutmeg, in the past, as today, is to spice both food and drink.

The hard kernel is exported whole, and grated by the user when required. In this way, none of the essential quality is wasted and the full flavour is imparted. Nowadays its use is confined largely to the kitchen, but from at least the seventeenth century a gentleman carried a nutmeg in his pocket to be readily available when required. In particular, it was grated on punch, caudle, posset and other beverages.

Pocket-sized silver boxes were made from the late seventeenth century and were devised to contain a small grater as well as the nutmeg; the size of many of the surviving boxes suggesting that the kernel must have been halved or quartered in order to fit inside or that the boxes are mis-named. Shapes vary from cylinders, two to three inches long, to complex double-lidded boxes. The first-named variety have pull-off lids and contain tubular silver graters, while the outer cases are sometimes pierced. Like that of other strong-smelling spices and herbs, the aroma was thought in the past to be an effective preventive of the plague and other infectious diseases.

By the mid-eighteenth century many nutmeg graters were indistinguishable externally from snuff boxes, and only on opening them to reveal the steel grater could they be told apart. As with snuff boxes, there is a wide range of shapes, some decorated and many quite plain except for moulded rims. Some of the designs are most ingenious, and the makers include Phipps and Robinson and Hester Bateman, of London, and Samuel Pemberton and Matthew Linwood, of Birmingham.

A grater is sometimes found together with a corkscrew in a single silver container, and in this form may once have been part·of a canteen. Travellers or picknickers have been the people most likely to want these two devices so conveniently and compactly packaged.

PAP BOATS

The pap boat is a small-sized bowl shaped especially for the feeding of infants. It is shallow, oval and tapers at one end so that whatever it contains can be introduced into an eager (or a reluctant) mouth by gently tipping the vessel. Silver ones have survived from the early eighteenth century onwards.

They have been found a modern use by smokers, who employ them as pipe-rests or as ashtrays. Fraudulently, they have been given feet and a handle to appear at the table as sauce boats, but as they are normally much smaller in size than genuine ones the deception will only hoodwink the inexperienced.

PORRINGERS

A porringer is a vessel from which, strictly speaking, porridge was eaten, and its name was formerly applied to what have become known as two-handled cups. The latter may also have been employed for the same purpose, but there is no firm evidence on the point.

The one-time porringer is a flat bowl with one or two flat ear-like handles, of which the one-handled type used to be called a bleeding bowl. The lurid name conjures up pictures of wealthy old English gentlemen letting their blood trickle into good polished silver, and possibly this vision may have encouraged their sale to romantically-minded collectors.

Porringers came into use in the late seventeenth century, and were made for a few decades. The majority of them are quite plain except for the handles or handle, which was given pierced decoration. This is usually neatly finished but heavy in design, as to have made it delicate would have weakened the handle and rendered it useless.

There are references in old documents to silver 'caudle cups' and 'posset pots', but it has proved difficult to identify them. There was no standard practice at the time as to what liquid or food should be taken from a particular vessel, and people doubtless pleased themselves. A line in a Will about 'my old silver caudle cup' could refer to the cup especially favoured by the testator for the purpose, and might well have been a trophy he won at racing.

Caudle and posset were very popular drinks made with gruel and milk respectively, both being flavoured with ale or wine and spices. English pottery posset pots, made at Lambeth and Bristol in about 1700, have two upright looped handles and a curved spout, like that of a teapot, through which the contents could be sucked or poured. A few comparable vessels in silver have been noted as surviving.

PUNCH BOWLS

Punch was a drink introduced into England in the early part of the seventeenth century by Englishmen who had been in the East. It could be made in a variety of ways, but Dr Johnson in 1756 quoted Jonathan Swift as the authority for its definition as

A liquor made by mixing spirit with water, sugar, and the juice of lemons.

Half a century earlier, William Salmon gave clear instructions in his *Family Dictionary*, which are:

Take two quarts wanting half a pint of Water, half a pint of Lime Juice; the juice of a Limon and four Oranges squeez'd in; and also three quarters of a pound of fine sugar; mix these altogether and strain it thro' a fine Strainer; so do three times till it be very clear: Then put to it a quart of Brandy (and a pint of White-wine if you please) and so proportionable for any quantity. If you put in a pint of White-wine, there must be two quarts of Water, and more Sugar in proportion to that addition.

The same author gives a further recipe which contains, among other ingredients, 'seven or eight drops of the true Spirit of Salt, and a dram of Alkernes, or two grains of Musk, and three of Ambergrice'. In addition it contained a whole grated nutmeg, and was topped by toasted bread. It is supposed to have derived its name from the Hindustani word *panch*, meaning five, in allusion to the number of ingredients in the original drink.

Fig. 59
Punch bowl on moulded pedestal foot. By David Willaume, 1730. Diameter 10¼ inches. Weight 63 oz. 14 dwt.

Silver punch bowls measure an average of 12 inches in diameter, but exceptional examples are known. Of these, the largest, made in 1726, has a diameter of 19 inches and a capacity of four gallons. It belongs to Jesus College, Oxford, to which it was presented in 1732.

The bowls were made from about 1680, and were each raised on a low moulded foot with or without a band of gadrooning. If decoration is present it usually takes the form of an engraved coat of arms, and an occasional bowl has a pair of handles. Porcelain bowls were imported from China in ever-increasing quantities as the century progressed, and by about 1740 the silver ones were virtually no longer being made.

see **MONTEITHS**

PUNCH LADLES

The long-stemmed ladle was made in large numbers, for its use was not restricted to silver bowls and it would have served its purpose equally well with vessels of pottery, porcelain or glass. The handle is usually found to have been made from whalebone, varying in colour from grey to black, with a silver tip and an oval or circular bowl. Frequently the bowl is inset with a silver coin which may provide a clue to the date of manufacture, because the ladles are only occasionally marked. Ladles of more ambitious pattern were made, but are scarce.

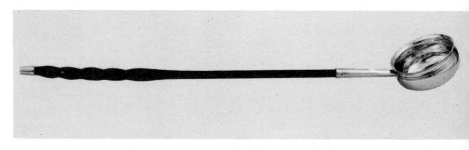

Fig. 60
Punch ladle with a handle of twisted whalebone. By Simon Jouet, 1737. Length 15 inches.

QUAICHS

The quaich (or quaigh) is a shallow two-handled drinking bowl used in Scotland, with a name adapted from the Gaelic. Silver examples were made during the late seventeenth century and the eighteenth century at Edinburgh and elsewhere north of the Border, and some of them are engraved in imitation of wood originals made from hooped wood staves

In some Scottish churches they serve as communion cups, and four of them at Ayr are hallmarked 1722. A large-sized example made at Edinburgh two years later, is at Donaldson's Hospital in that city. Another large one is used as an alms dish at a church in Banffshire.

SALT CELLARS

The salt cellar was introduced in the early seventeenth century, and was preceded by the standing salt; an object to which was attached considerable importance. Surviving specimens are among the most splendid examples of the silversmiths art, and the expression 'to sit above or below the salt', according to one's social status, demonstrates their ceremonial application.

While at first the great salt was placed on the long table so as to divide host and guests from other diners, it was later accompanied by small-sized individual salt-containers set by each plate. By the end of the seventeenth century the standing salt ceased to be made and the smaller variety, termed Trencher Salts, were in general use. They are round, oval, square or polygonal in shape, rest flat on the table with sides rising about $1\frac{1}{2}$ inches and with a central round or oval depression to hold the salt. Ornament takes the form of moulding at base and rim and often includes an engraved crest, although a few vary from this simple pattern. A gilt example in the Victoria and Albert Museum has narrow mouldings at top and base, while the bulged sides are shaped with ribs.

A change in the design had occurred by the mid-eighteenth century, when a round or oval bowl resting on three feet was in favour. The bowl itself was given decoration in the form of a gadrooned out-turned rim and perhaps swags of embossed and chased flowers, while the legs were often those of lions rising to lion masks where they joined the body of the article. This type stood a little higher than the earlier ones and the diameter averaged three inches, while the interiors were often gilded to prevent corrosion.

The decade 1760–70 saw the introduction of a fresh style which continued to maintain its popularity until the close of the century. Basically it was oval in shape and raised on four legs, instead of the former three, and the sides were pierced. The cut-out patterns were argumeted by engraving, which became bright cut after about 1780. To retain the salt they were fitted with liners of deep blue glass which showed through the openwork sides and emphasised their pattern.

After 1800 they were often made in the form of a bowl supported on a short pedestal, a form which had occasionally appeared before. There were also intermittent revivals of earlier varieties, providing something to suit every taste. Today, these salt cellars of late date are less expensive than earlier ones, and many of them are sufficiently pleasing in design to make acceptable substitutes.

Throughout the eighteenth and nineteenth centuries the salt cellar was made in multiples of two, and although occasionally a set of a dozen or more is recorded the greater proportion survive in pairs. They are articles still employed for their original purpose, and an odd one is not much sought after unless it is of exceptional interest. If that is the case, then it is wanted for the collector's cabinet rather than the dining table.

Fig. 61
Two of a set of four salt cellars with pierced sides and blue glass liners. By Hester Bateman, 1776. Width 3⅛ inches. Weight 5 oz. 15 dwt. (four).

SALVERS, TRAYS AND WAITERS

The salver, sometimes referred to as a tazza, is a small-sized tray for standing beneath a vessel containing liquid 'to save the Carpit or Cloathes from drips'. Prior to about 1720 they were given a centrally-placed capstan-shaped foot, which was sometimes made detachable. In many instances surviving examples have lost this appendage, but traces of it usually remain visible on the underside of the circular tray. This often has a gadrooned rim, matching similar ornament round the foot, and the centre is engraved with a coat of arms. After 1720, the tray has three of four short feet round the edge, the number depending on the shape of the piece.

While the salver was commonly placed under a tankard of beer or a container of some other beverage, it was also the forerunner of kettle and teapot stands. Its other uses were numerous, and in 1962 Sotheby's sold a pair of silver copies of Chinese porcelain ginger jars complete with their octagonal capstan-footed salvers, all engraved with Oriental scenes and hallmarked 1682. Later, in 1969, at Christie's was a coffee pot of 1739 accompanied by a tray made nine years later, the latter inscribed 'A Coffee Pot and Stand. The Gift of Mrs Arabella Hayes to Phillis Hooke'.

While many of the salvers and trays were for use, others were decorative and commemorative. In this category are the particularly fine ones made

Plate 13   114
(Top to bottom): Fiddle pattern teaspoon. Maker's mark G F, 1814.—Teaspoon with bright cut engraved decoration. By Charles Marsh, Dublin, 1825.—Mustard spoon. Maker's mark R B, 1809. Teaspoon By Thomas Wallis, 1797.—Salt shovel. By Peter and Ann Bateman, 1792. Length 4 inches.

from the Great Seal after it had been retained by retiring Lord Chancellors. The Walpole Salver of Sir Robert Walpole, made in 1728 by Paul de Lamerie and now in the Victoria and Albert Museum, is the supreme example of this practice. It is 19½ inches in width, square with incurved corners and a patterned rim, the centre and borders very probably engraved by William Hogarth before he took to painting (see page 43).

Large salvers were used for holding the tea equipage, and were sometimes accompanied by a wooden table of which the top was made especially to hold them. The top of such a table had spaces round the edge shaped to accept the feet of the salver, and the rim of the latter simulated carved wood. Thus, many salvers from about 1740 onwards have what is known as a 'pie-crust' edge; a pattern popularly linked with the mahogany furniture of Thomas Chippendale.

Fig. 62
Salver (or Tazza) raised on a turned foot and with a moulded rim. By David Willaume, 1720. Diameter 7 inches. Weight 17 oz. (pair).

From about 1770 there was a fashion for large oval trays, many of them with an upright pierced gallery having hand-holds cut out at opposite ends. Others, with a moulded rim were given open handles projecting outwards. From the turn of the century elaborately modelled and pierced borders were not uncommon, and some very large and handsome trays were made. The most sumptuous of them were gilded.

Plate 14   115
Pair of candlesticks. Maker's mark obliterated, 1702. Height 6¾ inches. Weight 12 oz. 10 dwt.

Fig. 63
One of a pair of trays with pierced
borders of drapery swags depending from
rams' heads and centred on vase medallions. Probably by William Cox, 1777.
Weight 82 oz. (pair).

In modern usage all three terms, salver, tray and waiter have become
interchangeable. At all periods they were carefully made and often bore
well-designed decoration, while usually ensuring that the latter did not
completely obstruct their function. The various styles of ornament were all
featured as they were fashionable, and the variations in pattern are
numerous.

Fig. 64
One of a pair of gilt oval trays with vine
leaf and grape borders, the centres engraved with coats of arms. By Digby
Scott and Benjamin Smith, 1805. Width
27¼ inches. Weight 376 oz. (pair).

SAUCEBOATS

Because there are so many hundreds of surviving sauce boats, both in
silver and porcelain, it would appear that our ancestors held sauces and
gravies in high esteem. Eighteenth century cookery books give plenty of
examples, and it is evident that much consideration was given to garnishing
a dish in order to accentuate its flavour. French sauces were famed, then
as now, and Hannah Glasse, whose *Art of Cookery* first appeared in 1747,
sternly warned her readers: 'Read this Chapter, and you will find how
expensive a French cook's sauce is'.

The earliest known English silver sauceboats date from the end of the
seventeenth century, but it would seem that they were very scarce before
about 1720. The earliest type is one of the most attractive in appearance,
while not necessarily the most practical in use. It is oval with a handle on
each of the long sides, is drawn out to a spout at either end and raised on

117

Fig. 65
One of a pair of oval double-lipped sauce
boats. By William Shaw, 1730. Length
about 8 inches. Weight 28 oz. 5 dwt.
(pair).

a low moulded foot. Like many other pieces of silver it was copied in
Chinese porcelain of the period, and is, in fact, less rare in that fragile
medium than it is in the precious metal.

By 1730 a different pattern was being made, and this one endured for
much of the rest of the century. Again, the shape was oval, but the spout
was at one end while the handle occupied the other. The decoration of the
rim varied between simple mouldings and complex designs incorporating
shells and other rococo motifs, while some examples were on a pedestal foot
and others had three or four short legs. The latter were single or complex
scrolls, ending in hoofs, paws and birdlike palmate extensions, while the
handles were no less various in pattern. Many were complete loops formed
of linked scrolls (Plate 7), but others curled upwards from the body of the
boat and did not join it again at the top; a type known as a 'flying scroll
handle'.

After 1760 the sauce boat began lost its individuality, and became a
miniature covered tureen matching in shape those provided for soup. They
had no pouring lips, so that their contents had to be served by means of a
ladle, and many were complete with a matching stand.

Fig. 66
Pair of sauce boats with moulded rims
and engraved bodies. By Paul de Lamerie,
1735. Weight 31 oz. (pair).

Fig. 67
Pair of sauce boats with reeded rims and
handles and rectangular bases. By Peter,
Ann and William Bateman, 1799.
Width 8¼ inches. Weight 23 oz. 10 dwt.
(pair).

Both sauce boats and sauce tureens were made in pairs and multiples of two, and an odd specimen is normally valued at less than 50% of the price of two.

SAUCEPANS AND SKILLETS

The skillet is a long-handled deep pan raised on three short legs to raise it above the source of heat. In the later seventeenth century it was sometimes made of silver, and some surviving specimens retain their covers. These are domed with a short flat pierced handle so that when reversed they could be used as bowls.

119

Fig. 68
Pair of sauce tureens and covers with
partly lobed bodies, gadrooned mouldings
and reeded loop handles to the lids.
Maker's mark TE.GS. Height about 6
inches. Weight 56 oz. (pair).

In the following century the silver saucepan replaced the skillet. Its shape
varied from time to time between the simple straight-sided and the 'bag-
shape', which bulges at the base (Plate 9). Some of the earlier ones have
their handles set at right-angles to a short spout, and later they were sold
complete with a stand holding a spirit lamp.

Nineteenth century saucepans of diminutive size were used for warming
brandy at the dinner-table, but the precise purpose of earlier ones is less
certain.

SCONCES

A sconce is the old name of what is popularly called today a wall-light.
The value of polished silver in reflecting the light of a candle was noted at
an early date, and candle-holders fixed before a shaped backplate were
known in the mid-sixteenth century. None have survived, nor have any of
the few later possessed by Charles I.

After the Restoration they became plentiful and the fifty years between
1660 and 1710 saw their heyday. A decade later, an inventory taken in 1721
records 210 sconces in the royal palaces, but it is thought that most, if not
all, would have been made at an earlier date. Of them, fourteen were of
silver constructed with a sheet of mirror-glass to act as a reflector, and their
weight is recorded as totalling 3,219 ounces.

The simplest type of sconce, of which a few examples have survived, has
a shaped backplate from which springs one or more arms with candle-

sockets. Their ornamentation was of a high quality, with the plates suitably shaped and sometimes also pierced. The embossing and chasing were usually bold and incorporated all the current motifs with swags of fruit,

Fig. 69
Saucepan with turned wood handle. By
Paul de Lamerie, 1717. Weight 7 oz.
(all in).

cupids and acanthus leaves in profusion. Many were made with the owner's crest or coronet as part of the design, while others make a central feature of a bold monogram.

A variant of this last type is one that is long and narrow in form, and perhaps made to hang on a pilaster. These owed their shape to France, and probably were introduced into England by the Huguenot silversmiths. The latter would not appear to have been their sole makers, because some are recorded with the marks of London-born craftsmen on them. This is not conclusive, however, because it is known that some of the foreign craftsmen, prior to receiving permission to establish themselves, handed their work to English silversmiths to be marked on their behalf. Such articles would, of course, bear the maker's stamp of the man actually

121

submitting them for assay, and would give no indication of their true origins.

Most surviving sconces weigh between thirty and one hundred ounces apiece. Typical of them is a pair in the Victoria and Albert Museum which were made in 1707 by David Willaume and weigh 76 oz. 10 dwt. A few years earlier the same silversmith, but under an anglicised name, supplied a pair to John Hervey, later first Earl of Bristol, who recorded his purchase in these words:

Paid David Williams . . . for a pair of chimney sconces all silver weighing 90 ounces 3 dwtt, at 7 shillings per ounce . . .

A month later, in February 1699 Hervey bought some more:

Paid David Williams for ye 8 great silver sconces weighing 491 ounces at 7 shilling per ounce & for graving etc., in all £175.

Today they would be valued at 50 or 60 times their cost.

SEAL BOXES

Important documents bear wax seals, sometimes measuring five or six inches in diameter, hanging from them by strong tapes. To protect the fragile wax from damage a silver box was sometimes provided. The boxes are circular with a close-fitting lid, the latter usually with a coat of arms in relief. Many seal boxes have been separated from the insignia they once guarded and are nowadays bought and sold for very different purposes from the original. Their most popular modern employment is to contain cigarettes.

SKEWERS

Silver skewers for meat have been in use since the early eighteenth century, but most old surviving examples date from the years around 1800. They measure a foot or so in length, and were given a variety of terminals. These often take the form of a cast shell or a plain or reeded ring, and they usually bear an engraved crest. With meat appearing at the table in smaller quantities than in the past, the skewer is now only seldom employed for its destined purpose. It has, however, acquired a modern use at which it is almost unbeatable: it makes an excellent paper knife (Plate 3).

Miniatures of the meat skewer, some 7 or 8 inches long, were made for game. These, too, open letters just as well as do the others.

SNUFFERS

The purpose of the pair of snuffers was to snuff a burning candle: i.e., to trim the wick. During the eighteenth century, before the introduction of plaited wicks, candles were a source of worry because they required continual attention while they were alight. The type of simple wick that was in use curled over as it burned and caused the candle to gutter: it melted rapidly and ran to waste while emitting black smoke and a bad smell.

Fig. 70
Snuffers with stand and candle-holder. Maker's mark W B with a mullet below, *circa* 1685. Height 7 inches. Weight 10 oz. 3 dwt.

The snuffers works like a pair of scissors, with loop handles and a central hinge, while the working end has a cutting blade with a small box to contain the waste ends of wick. The arm to which the box is affixed is extended to a point, which may be used to remove the stumps of candles from their sockets.

The earliest surviving pair of silver snuffers is in the British Museum. It bears the coats of arms of Christopher Bainbridge, Archbishop of York, and of King Henry VIII, and the insignia of the former includes a Cardinal's hat. This he received in 1512, and as he died two years later the snuffers can be dated between those years. Another pair, in the Victoria and Albert

123

Museum, is equally interesting. It bears the arms of Edward VI, who reigned from 1547 to 1553, and is inscribed: *God save Kynge Edwarde wythe all his Noble Covncel.*

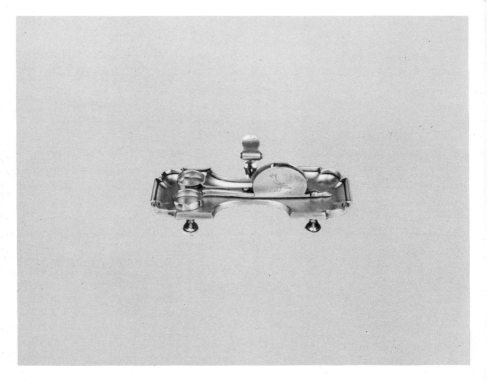

Fig. 71
Snuffer and shaped tray. By William Gould, 1792. Width 6¾ inches. Weight 10 oz. 13 dwt.

Snuffers from the late seventeenth century onwards are less scarce than the early ones mentioned. Each was equipped with a stand in the form of a short-stemmed candlestick supporting a rectangular or rounded oblong holder; in this the snuffers rested upright while a small hole allowed the pointed blade to protrude. Some of the stands were complete with a conical extinguisher, and a few exceptional examples also had a taper stick. In both instances the appendages hooked on by means of square pegs which fitted into slots shaped to receive them.

From the first quarter of the eighteenth century this upright pattern of stand was replaced by a flat tray or pan. It was shaped sometimes exactly to the snuffers, but otherwise was usually oblong with curved ends and in both instances had a handle midway along one side. Three short turned legs were fitted to the snuffers, so that it stood neatly.

The snuffers usually bore little ornament beyond an engraved crest or coat of arms. The tray was given more decoration, and often had a moulded rim and engraved border, while the handle varied between plain linked scrolls and elaborate curling acanthus leaves.

It is not uncommon to find that the late seventeenth century pairs of snuffers are marked with a maker's stamp different from that on the stand. A probable explanation of this is that the makers of snuffers were specialists who made little else, while the stands were part of the normal output of others or of general silversmiths. In spite of having come from separate workshops, if both pieces bear the same old engraved insignia it is usually accepted that they have always been together.

More than one snuffer tray has been converted at some time into a more useful, and more saleable, inkstand by the addition of an inkwell and a pounce pot. It is a type of faking that is not always easy to detect, especially when the marks on the added items appear to match those on the tray.

SOAP BOXES

Soap was supplied in the form of a ball, so boxes for its reception were in the same shape but raised on a low foot for stability. They opened centrally and the lids were pierced in a manner comparable to the caster, usually with the additional embellishment of engraving. They are now rare.

SPOONS

The importance of a spoon as an aid to feeding, and thus to the main-tenance of life, has always caused it to be treated with regard. In medieval times the majority of the people in England used spoons made of wood or horn, but the existence of silver ones is recorded in documents and confirmed by some surviving specimens. A will of 1259 mentions twelve silver spoons, and a number of eleventh century examples are in museums in England and Scotland. As they have decorated handles and bowls it is not unlikely that, like the famous and slightly later Coronation spoon, they were for ceremonial use.

By the fifteenth century a number of distinctive types had made their appearance and remained popular until the Restoration. Although they are admittedly outside the scope of this book because of their date, they played their part in the development of the spoon and a brief notice of them may not be without interest. Also, some of them are comparatively un-common, and may well come the way of a collector.

In each instance the bowl is what has been described aptly as 'fig-shaped', with the narrow end joined to the stem or stalk. The variation between one and another is seen in the termination of the stem, which was finished in a number of ways. The ends, known as knops, were often finished with gilding, and their patterns include:

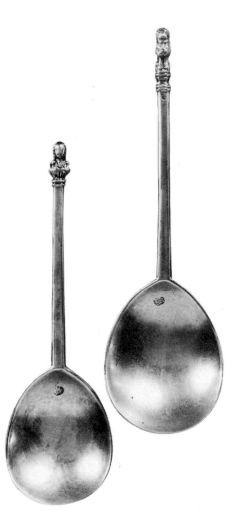

Fig. 72
(Left) Maidenhead terminal and (right) Lion sejant. Late sixteenth century. Lenght about 5 inches.

126

Acorn: with the cup joining the stem and the fruit uppermost.

Diamond-point: with a pointed diamond-shaped terminal.

Lion sejant: with a seated lion, placed either full-face or with its body at right-angles and its head turned to the front.

Maidenhead: with the head and shoulders of a woman, perhaps originally meant as a representation of the Virgin Mary.

Moor's head: with the head of a curly-haired man.

Puritan: mid-seventeenth century; with a flat handle widening towards the top, which is sometimes finished with two curved notches and a short line dividing them.

Seal: with a flat circular top above a baluster which is sometimes ornamented with ribs or gadrooning. Many variations in detail occur.

Slip: the stem is cut at the top at an angle, appearing as if it had been sliced with a sharp knife.

Woodwose: with the 'wild man of the woods' who is shown with his club.

Wrythen: with an egg-shaped knob spirally fluted.

The best-known of all are the Apostle spoons, which were made in sets and singly. The sets comprise the twelve Apostles, with a thirteenth which is either Christ or St. Paul; each shown bearing his attribute and wearing an outsize halo. They were frequently given as christening presents, and while a rich donor might contribute a full set on such an occasion it was more common for a child to receive just one. It might bear the effigy of the Saint after whom he or she was named or to whom he or she was dedicated, or perhaps the patron Saint of the giver.

Complete sets of the spoons are excessively rare, but single specimens are less difficult to acquire. Many of them are marked on both front and back of the bowl and on the stem, but no hard and fast rules can be given. The spoons were made in both London and the provinces, and the marks used in some of the smaller towns have been the subject of considerable research. The standard work on the subject is by the late Commander G. E. P. How and Mrs J. P. How, and is entitled *English and Scottish Silver Spoons*. It runs to three volumes published between 1952 and 1957.

Quite soon after the Restoration of the monarchy in 1660 a new style of spoon began to be made, and continued to be produced for several decades. The flat stem is made to taper to a point, the so-called 'rat tail', raised on the back of the bowl which is an almost perfect oval. The top of the stem is broadened, rounded and given two 'V'-shaped nicks, which earned it the

127

name of trifid or trefid: meaning split into three.

The marking of trifids is more regular than that of earlier spoons, but many remain debatable. The flat stem was often used for adding initials and a date by or for the owner. They are 'pricked' by forming them from a succession of tiny dots or pricks, and failing a punched date a contemporary pricked one is generally an acceptable second-best.

Fig. 73
(Left) 'Dognose' with rat-tail on the bowl, probably by Benjamin Watts, 1704.
(Right) Trefid, probably Lincoln, *circa* 1680.

128

By about 1710 the notches in the terminal had become less definite, the whole was rounded and resembled three hillocks of which the centre one was taller than the others. This 'wavy' end was then replaced by one completely rounded at the corners and given an upward curl with a central short rib, while the shape of the bowl remained unaltered and retained the decorative reinforcement of the rat tail.

The latter was generally discontinued after 1730, although it was still made for those who wanted it, and by the mid-century the Old English pattern had evolved. It has a stem broadening to a rounded top, like the preceding type, but curling down and thickening at the end. The bowl is egg-shaped, and reinforced on the underside with one or more round-ended flattened 'drops'.

At about the same date (c. 1750) there was a brief vogue for the 'Onslow' pattern. This acquired its name from Arthur Onslow, who served as Speaker of the House of Commons from 1728 to 1761. The pattern of handle bearing his name has a downcurved end which terminates in a wide ribbed scroll.

After 1760 the Old English style, while retaining its outline, was given decorative additions in the form of patterned edgings. They were narrow borders of beading, reeding or engraved bright cut feathering; the latter simulating cast gadrooning. Towards the end of the century, such ornament increased and usually centred on a space for a crest or a monogram.

In the early nineteenth century the widely popular 'Fiddle' pattern, which has a silhouette resembling that of a violin, was introduced. Later, came the equally long-lived 'King's' pattern, with its combination of scrolls and anthemion topped by a shell.

The spoons made prior to 1700 were much of a size, although they varied from time to time between 5 and 7 inches in length. After that year they started to be produced according to their intended use; and before long it was possible to buy tablespoons, dessertspoons and teaspoons in matching patterns. In addition, from then onwards, there were increasing numbers for particular purposes, which included:

Basting: long-handled over-sized spoons were made from about 1700.

Straining: known alternatively as Gravy spoons, these large-sized spoons were pierced so that any solid matter was retained and the pure gravy could be poured from them.

Serving: in size between Basting and Table spoons, these were used as their name indicates.

Mustard: known to have existed in the late seventeenth century but none before the mid-eighteenth century have been preserved. They are usually in the form of small-sized ladles, with a circular deep bowl and a slightly curled handle (Plate 13).

Salt: early eighteenth century examples are miniatures of ordinary spoons. They were followed by some in the shape of a ladle and others with a bowl in the form of a shovel (Plate 13).

Snuff: miniatures of ordinary spoons were made during the eighteenth century for keeping inside a box to assist in taking snuff.

See **CADDY SPOONS**
    MARROW SCOOPS
    STRAINERS

STANDING CUPS

The standing cup and cover raised on a tall stem and foot was a highly-prized possession from the sixteenth century. Intended rather for display than for use, considerable skill was exercised in its design and making. Patterns of many English silver examples were based on the work of German artists, and many splendid specimens have been preserved.

The cups continued to be made until shortly after the Restoration, when they were supplanted by the vase-shaped covered cup supported on a low foot and with two handles. This annexed the social function of the standing cup, and grew from the two-handled porringer which had come into use in the mid-seventeenth century.

See **TWO-HANDLED CUPS**
    PORRINGERS

STIRRUP CUPS

The stirrup cup is for holding a drink to be taken while mounted on horseback, usually prior to a hunt moving off. As it is of small capacity it can be emptied quickly and there is no need to set it down during use, which would be an impossibility anyway, while in the saddle. The most popular surviving late eighteenth/early nineteenth century specimens are those in the shape of a fox's head. Modelled in detail, the fur is represented realistically and they are of a size to be held easily in the hand. Contemporary counterparts in porcelain were made at the Derby factory and elsewhere.

STRAINERS

A few seventeenth century strainers have been preserved, and have round bowls with long tapering handles. From the following century they survive

Plate 15   130
Teapot. By Hannah Northcote, 1798. Height 4⅝ inches. Weight 8 oz. 3 dwt. (all in).—Strawberry dish. By David King, Dublin, 1745. Diameter 4¾ inches. Weight 2 oz. 15 dwt.

in larger numbers, as might be expected. Each has a circular bowl pierced with holes, often in an elaborate and attractive pattern, and a pair of flat scrolled handles. Having been intended for use with oranges and lemons in the making of punch, they are of a large size when compared with the modern tea strainer.

A strainer resembling a teaspoon, but with the bowl pierced and with a pointed terminal is known as a 'mote skimmer'. This is presumably because it could be used to skim motes, or impurities, from a liquid. They date from the eighteenth century and were used at the tea table, the spike on the handle being employed to free the teapot spout if it became blocked.

A few churches include among their plate skimmers designed with appropriate emblems cast or engraved on their handles, which were for straining the communion wine. In some instances secular mote skimmers are found similarly employed, as are silver sugar sifters.
See **MAZARINES**

STRAWBERRY DISHES

Circular dishes, measuring from four to five inches in diameter and with upcurved rims which are shaped and ribbed, are usually called strawberry dishes. Their pleasing name is doubtless a modern one, but it is not improbable that they were made to hold fruit of some kind, if not strawberries. Larger-sized dishes of the same pattern were possibly for serving, and may have formed part of a set.

The dishes were made in Ireland during the first quarter of the eighteenth century, and in England during the same period as well as earlier (Plate 15).

SUGAR BASINS

It is thought that sugar was taken with tea from early in the eighteenth century, and that is was brought to the table in a small basin Among the earliest of silver examples used for the purpose is a bowl of normal type with a cover fitting loosely inside the rim. The cover is domed with a raised rim round the centre of the top, resulting in an appearance similar to that of an inverted saucer. The pattern is paralleled in contemporaneous Chinese porcelain and in later Pekin glass, and the cover with its awkward hand-grip may have been stood upside down to serve as a spoon tray. The basins were generally circular and occasionally polygonal, but both varieties are rare and there does not seem to have been a standard design.

From about 1740 sugar was kept in a container matching the two used for tea, and all three were stored in a wood box. Then, about 1760 separate sugar bowls were again made. In some instances they are boat-shaped, in others they resemble vases, and most of them are pierced and fitted with blue glass liners (see page 27).

Plate 16   131
Tureen and cover of rococo design. By John Edwards, 1744. Width 16½ inches. Weight 114 oz.

Finally, at the end of the century, when teasets comprising matched articles were being made, the sugar basin followed the lines of the teapot and cream jug.

Fig. 74.
Octagonal sugar basin with domed cover. By Richard Watts, 1712. Height 5¼ inches.

Fig. 75
Octagonal sugar basin, the domed cover with a raised rim. By T. Tearle, 1730. Height about 3 inches.

SUGAR TONGS

Part of the silver equipage of the well-appointed tea table was a pair of tongs for handling the sugar. They were of two patterns: the scissor and the spring arm (Plate 11). The scissor variety is similar in conception to the familiar pair of cutters, with a central hinge and ring handles for the fingers. They were designed as a series of linked scrolls, the grips were usually cast in the shape of scallop-shells, and they probably date from the mid-eighteenth century. Only a small proportion of those found bear a full set of marks, and to name the precise year of making is usually not possible. They are sometimes referred to as sugar nips.

From about 1755 onwards spring-back tongs gradually superseded the others. Early examples were given arms ornamented with piercing, but later they were left solid. The grips were almost invariably in the shape of small spoons, with the arms slightly incurved at the edges. Many of the later ones were given engraved bright cut decoration of the usual type, and the stamp of Hester Bateman is not infrequently on them. Again, a full set of marks is not always found, and they must more often be dated by style than by date-letter.

SWEETMEAT BASKETS

Small-sized baskets of oval or circular shape were used for holding sweetmeats from about 1740, and have cast as well as pierced decoration. Later, the piercing was used less often and replaced by engraving. The baskets were often suspended from the arms of an épergne, of which they formed a part, but it is likely that they were also sold separately.

TANKARDS

It was Sydney Smith, the nineteenth century cleric and wit, who inquired 'What two ideas are more inseparable than Beer and Britannia?', and to many people some of the finest English silver is to be found in the form of beer tankards. While specimens dating from the sixteenth century have been preserved, they are so very few in number as to be beyond the range of most collectors.

A pair of particularly fine Elizabethan tankards, hallmarked 1602 and of silver-gilt, was sold by Christie's in 1966. Each is of tapering cylindrical shape with both the foot and the domed cover embossed and chased with groups of fruit. The body is engraved with a pattern of scrolled strapwork and leaves on a matted ground, which is repeated on the handle. They stand $8\frac{1}{4}$ inches high and although other tankards of the period are known, only two pairs, of which this is one, have been recorded. When they were sold by auction in 1962 they realised £9,200 ($25,760), and four years later they changed hands again for £17,000 ($47,600).

Fig. 76
Tankard with tapering cylindrical body
and flat-topped lid, engraved with
Oriental figures. Maker's mark W A in
monogram, 1683. Height 4 inches.
Weight 9 oz. 4 dwt.

134

While seventeenth century silver tankards are certainly more plentiful than those of earlier periods, they are keenly sought and consequently expensive. They are mostly of plain form, again with a tapering cylindrical body, but with a flat-topped cover (see pages 21 and 40). Decoration is largely confined to a moulding round the base and rim and to variations in the design of the thumbpiece: the upright lever set over the hinge for lifting the cover. Occasional examples are engraved with Chinese-inspired scenes, and nearly all have a scrolled handle ending in a small shaped plate.

Fig. 77
Tankard with domed lid and moulded base. Probably by Francis Hoyte, 1709. Height about 6¼ inches. Weight 22 oz.

An exceptional pair of the last-mentioned type engraved with Chinamen among trees and birds, hallmarked 1686, was sold by Christie's in 1963 for £17,000 ($47,600). They re-appeared in the same saleroom in November 1968, and in that short interval their value had appreciated to no less than £56,000 ($134,400). It must be emphasised, however, that this pair of tankards was as outstanding in its way as the pair described above. A single specimen will be found to fetch considerably less than half as much as a pair, as the supply of the latter is extremely limited. Such extraordinary prices make exciting reading, but above all they demonstrate that the finest and rarest of silver is unquestionably a good investment.

135

Fig. 77A
Tankard with a scroll thumbpiece and
domed lid, engraved on the body with a
jockey mounted on a racehorse and in-
scribed 'The Duke of Somerset's Plate att
Midhurst ye 28th Day of May 1713. By
Richard Green, 1712. Height 9¼ inches.
Weight 40 oz.

136

Fig. 78
'The Cumberland Tankard', of outstanding weight, size and capacity, and engraved with a view of the battle of Culloden, at which the Duke of Cumberland was the victorious general. The thumbpiece is in the form of a lion, and the same animals holding castors between their paws form the feet so that the article might be passed round a table—perhaps at a regimental mess. By Gabriel Sleath, 1746. Height 12¾ inches. Weight 114 oz.

Fig. 79
Tankard with tucked-in base and double scroll handle. Probably by W. and R. Peaston, 1763. Height about 6½ inches. Weight 9 oz.

The more usual thumbpiece patterns to be found on tankards are cast scrolls rising to a horizontal corkscrew, while others include figures of lions and crossed pomegranates: both sometimes also forming the feet of the vessels. Such embellishments are comparatively rare, and the majority of examples have a moulded edge around the base.

Almost all the tankards of the late seventeenth century have what is by modern standards a large capacity. It can be as much as five pints, which suggests either that the beer once served was a weaker brew or that the heads and stomachs of our ancestors were considerably stronger than ours.

Fig. 80
Tankard with flat lid, the body engraved with two bands of reeding. By Septimus and James Crespell, 1771. Height 6¾ inches. Weight 29 oz. 4 dwt.

Some examples are fitted internally with a vertical row of short pegs, and are referred to as 'peg tankards'. The purpose of these marks was to gauge the amount of drink consumed on convivial occasions when the vessel was passed round the company. Each guest was required to drink exactly a peg's-worth and no more, and it had to be done at a draught. If the quantity was exceeded, then he had to continue to the next one. It was this daunting little game which gave rise to the well-known expression about taking someone 'down a peg'.

During the first decades of the eighteenth century the shape of the tankard began to alter. It grew taller and less in diameter than before, the lower part of the body curved in and then swelled out to form a shallow moulded base, and the cover was domed. At the same time, the scrolls forming the handle became more complicated, and a large 'C' curve linked to a reversed small one was common.

By 1750 rococo curves were reflected in the design, and the body was of baluster shape. The cover remained domed, and the moulded foot was made a little taller than before. Handles continued to be a combination of curves, and were frequently capped by a leaf.

In the last part of the century there was a liking for barrel-shaped tankards, and these were often engraved with bands of reeding resembling the iron hoops on wooden barrels. The cover was made flat or domed according to taste, and it is usual to find that the average capacity has diminished until it is in the region of a single pint.

A large number of surviving old tankards are engraved with coats of arms, and it is not at all rare for them to be mentioned in wills and treated as heirlooms. While they were doubtless used from time to time, it is probable that many of them were commemorative objects and were treated with due care. Thus, quite a number are in remarkably good condition considering their age, and should continue to give pleasure by their appearance and function for many centuries to come.

TAPER BOXES

Wax for sealing letters and documents in the eighteenth century was often melted by a lighted length of flexible wax taper. It could be kept and used either in a taper box or on a wax jack. The former can have a handle by which the taper is wound and unwound on an axle, or is a simple cylindrical container in which it is loosely coiled. In either case the lid has a central hole with a raised funnel-like rim through which the taper emerges. Some of the boxes have a small conical extinguisher attached to them by a chain, and are additionally fitted with a handle. Most of them are plain little articles for a utilitarian purpose, and today are interesting because of the function they once performed. They were made throughout the eighteenth century, but early examples are understandably the most scarce (Plate 9).

see **WAX JACKS**

139

TAPER STICKS

Small-sized candles were sometimes used at the writing-desk for melting wax when a letter had to be sealed. To hold the candles miniature candlesticks, known as taper sticks, were in use from the late seventeenth century onwards. They were of two kinds: those similar to a normal full-size table candlestick, and those on a flat base like a chamber candlestick.

The former variety survives in large numbers, and can be found aping its bigger brothers in each successive style. Those in the plain patterns favoured during the reigns of Queen Anne and George I are particularly attractive to modern taste, and are eagerly sought. The flat-based taper stick again followed the designs of its full-size prototype, and, like it, was usually equipped with a conical extinguisher. In exceptional instances it also had a pair of snuffers.

Many eighteenth century inkstands, of both silver and porcelain have a taper stick as their central feature.

See **TAPER BOXES** and **WAX JACKS**

TEA CADDIES

Prior to the end of the eighteenth century what we now term a tea caddy was known as a tea canister. The later name is a distortion of the Malay word '*kati*': standing for a weight of about 1⅓ lbs. by which tea was sold in the East. The canister was used in the late seventeenth century, but examples of that date are extremely rare, and it is from Queen Anne's time that rather more have been preserved. Then, they were oval or oblong in shape, the latter with and without cut corners, with a short neck and a domed cover; types copied in the Far East and included with Chinese porcelain teasets for some decades to come. In order to make the silver examples easier to fill many of them were made with sliding removable bases.

Throughout the century the caddies were usually sold in sets of two or three fitted in a lockable box of mahogany, or of some other wood covered in panels of carved mother-of-pearl, black shagreen or tortoiseshell. Many of the boxes bear silver corner mounts, handles, escutcheons and feet, which were only occasionally hallmarked. Two of the caddies were for containing black (or 'Bohea') and green teas, and the third, if present, held sugar. Towards the end of the century the third container was dispensed with and replaced by a glass bowl.

The two types of tea were the cause of much confusion in botanical circles, and their origin was frequently debated. Throughout the eighteenth century it was thought that they came from completely different plants, named by Linnaeus *Thea bohea* and *Thea viridis*. The truth was not known

140

until about 1850, when Robert Fortune returned from an expedition undertaken on behalf of the Horticultural Society of London. In a book recording his travels he wrote:

> . . . the black and green teas which generally come to England from the northern provinces of China are made from the same species, and the difference of colour, flavour, &c., is solely the result of the different modes of preparation.

Fig. 81
Octagonal tea caddy with domed cover, engraved with a monogram within leaf, shell and strapwork mantling. By Humphrey Payne, *circa* 1715. Height about 4 inches.

Fig. 82
Set of two caddies and a sugar box
ornamented with flowers, leaves and
scrolls and with oval panels of Oriental
scenes. By Paul de Lamerie, 1742 and
1744. Height 5⅜ inches. Weight 41 oz.

The custom of keeping tea-leaves under lock and key stemmed from the days when it was first imported and was very expensive. The old habit endured in spite of the fact that the price gradually fell during the course of the eighteenth century. Whether the keys were actually used in every instance is possibly debatable, but they were certainly provided for those who wanted to safeguard their little hoard. The fact that the caddy and contents were easily portable, locked or otherwise, would point to the likelihood that security was little more than a pretence.

The shape of the caddy changed from time to time, and from the simplicity of c. 1710 it became a bulging rectangle, a short vase and then an oval with a flat or a domed hinged lid. This last type was given a lock and the interior was usually divided into compartments.

Ornament was often lavishly applied, and everything from elaborate embossing and chasing to formal bright cut engraving appears on caddies. As the leaf was imported from China it is appropriate that mock-Oriental designs abounded, especially in the mid-century when the rococo style favoured them for everything. Knobs in the shape of tea-plant twigs are not uncommon, and some of the caddies bear on them Chinese characters.

142

On one such specimen in the Victoria and Albert Museum, hallmarked 1773, they have been translated and read 'upper', 'spring' and 'direction'; words that are quite meaningless in their context, but were doubtless copied only for decoration.

Fig. 83
Inlaid mahogany box with silver mounts, fitted with a pair of tea caddies ornamented with rams' heads, swags of leaves and other neo-classical motifs. By Pierre Gillois, 1776. Weight of caddies 36 oz. 10 dwt.

One of the most complete of recorded sets of caddies comprises three decorated with patterns in relief and engraved with coats of arms, twelve teaspoons, a mote skimmer, sugar-nips, cream jug and two knives. The caddies are by Paul de Lamerie, hallmarked 1735, and the other pieces except for the nips probably also came from his workshop. All are contained in a fitted mahogany box with silver mounts and a silver key.

143

Fig. 84
Double caddy with hinged covers and a
reeded handle, the body decorated with
formal engraving. By Henry Chawner,
1795. Height about 6½ inches. Weight
15 oz. 10 dwt.

TEAPOTS

A Chinese legend relates that the Emperor Chinnung discovered the social and medicinal virtues of tea in the year 2737 B.C., and other traditions indicate that the leaf was known and used for many centuries prior to its arrival in Europe. There are mentions of it in a few Italian and Dutch books and letters of the late sixteenth century, and some were translated into English and published.

The earliest printed reference to tea appeared in the form of an advertisement in the journal, *Mercurius Politicus* in September 1658. It ran:

That excellent and by all Physitians approved China Drink called by the Chineans Tcha, by other nations Tay, alias Tee, is sold at the Sultaness Head, a cophee-house in Sweeting Rents, by the Royal Exchange, London.

Very soon after the above notice appeared, Thomas Garway, proprietor of Garraway's Coffee-house in Change Alley, Cornhill, issued a hand-bill which stated that

144

Tea in England hath been sold in the leaf for six pounds, and some-times for ten pounds the pound weight, and in respect of its former scarceness and dearness, it hath been only used as a regalia in high treatments and entertainments, and presents made thereof to princes and grandees till the year 1651. The said Thomas Garway did pur-chase a quantity thereof, and first publicly sold the said tea in leaf and drink, made according to the directions of the most knowing merchants and travellers into those Eastern countries . . . and to the end that all persons of eminence and quality, gentlemen, and others, who have occasion for tea in leaf, may be supplied, these are to give notice that the said Thomas Garway hath tea to sell from sixteen to fifty shillings per pound.

Indulgence in the leaf must have grown with rapidity, because the very first Act of Parliament passed following the Restoration took notice of it. The House of Commons acted predictably and levied

on every gallon of chocolate, sherbet and tea, made and sold, to be paid by the maker thereof, eightpence.

However, Samuel Pepys was one London citizen who had not become addicted to it, for on 25th September of the same year as the Act was passed, 1660, he wrote in his diary that 'I did send for a cup of tea, a China drink, of which I never drunk before.'

So much for the leaf and its arrival in England, but how it was prepared for drinking is less certain. Two methods were known: the Japanese ground the dried leaf to powder, added hot water and drank the mixture, while the Chinese employed the method that remains usual today. They poured hot water on the prepared leaf while it was in a pot, and then drank the resulting decoction from cups.

Teapots made of red stoneware, a hard variety of pottery, were imported from China with the leaf, and acquired a reputation for brewing the best tea. There is also in the Victoria and Albert Museum a silver teapot dating from 1670. These all suggest that by that date people favoured steeping the leaf, rather than grinding it and drinking what a critic has described as 'a thin mixture of spinach and water.'

The 1670 teapot could easily be mistaken for a coffee-pot. It stands $13\frac{1}{2}$ inches in height, has a tapering cylindrical body and a hinged cover of conical shape with a knob on top. The leather-covered handle is set at right-angles to the spout, and the latter is a short straight tube emerging about one-third of the way down the body. Proof of its original purpose, in spite of its appearance to the contrary, is contained in the inscription engraved on the pot. It reads

This silver tea-Pott was presented to ye Comtee of ye East India Cumpany by ye Honoue George Lord Berkeley of Berkeley Castle

A member of that Honourable & worthy Society and A true Hearty Lover of them 1670

So far as is known this is an exceptional piece, as no others of the same form can be proved to have been intended for use with tea. It seems not improbable that an actual coffee-pot was selected for the reason that nothing else of silver was then in existence.

Two surviving pre-1700 teapots are egg-shaped, and made in imitation of Chinese wine-pots of the period. Both are gilt, and the earlier of the two, which dates to *c*. 1685 with the maker's mark of Richard Hoare is chased with vertical ribs dividing matted panels. The other, by Benjamin Pyne and perhaps a few years later in date, is hexagonal but with similar ribs and panels. Both have curved spouts with tiny hinged covers, and their hinged domed lids have decorative thumbpieces like those of contemporary tankards.

Fig. 85
Teapot of pear-shape with a domed lid and curved spout. By Pentecost Symonds, Exeter, 1712. Height 6 inches. Weight 16 oz. 5 dwt. (all in).

The reigns of Queen Anne and George I saw the making of teapots of which surviving specimens are both scarce and valuable. This latter is not due, as Mr Charles Oman points out, simply to their rarity, but is attributable to their beauty. At no subsequent date have they been surpassed, and few later examples have equalled their satisfying lines.

They are pear-shaped and either smooth or, more rarely, octagonal, with a tall curved spout. In a few instances the wood handle is set at right-angles, but this was no doubt found to be awkward in using such a squat article, and the majority of pots have it straight in line with the spout. The domed cover is hinged, and there is often a subsidiary cover to prevent any of the valued fragrance-laden vapour escaping from the spout-end.

Fig. 86
Gold 'bullet' or 'skittle-ball' teapot with straight spout and moulded foot, presented by George II as a prize at Leith races in 1736. By James Ker, Edinburgh, *circa* 1736. Length about 7 inches. Weight 20 oz. 4 dwt. (all in).

147

Some of these teapots retain their contemporary stands and spirit burners, and it is possible that all had them originally. This suggests either that our forefathers did not mind having their tea 'stewed', or that they brewed it in the Japanese manner. That being so, the teapots would have been used in the manner of kettles, but there appears to be no positive evidence on the point.

Fig. 87
Teapot of inverted pear shape, with a moulded foot and cast spout. By Thomas Whipham, 1754. Weight 18 oz. 5 dwt. (all in).

A painting of about 1720 in the Victoria and Albert Museum shows a lady and gentleman and a child taking tea, with the silver equipage clearly depicted. There is a teapot on a stand of the type just described, a tall covered jug, a tea-caddy, a covered sugar bowl, a waste bowl and a small tray with spoons. It does not indicate how the tea was brewed, and the tall jug, although resembling a modern one for hot water might equally have held milk.

148

The pear-shaped teapot remained fashionable for about twenty years, from *c*. 1700 to 1720, but during the second half of that period a fresh type began to appear. It was sometimes completely spherical, but most often slightly wider and flatter at the top than at the base. It is frequently referred to as a 'bullet' teapot, and is probably the best known of all those made in the eighteenth century.

Fig. 88
Teapot of oval shape with a long straight spout, the body decorated with bright cut engraving. By Peter and Ann Bateman, 1797. Width 10¼ inches. Matching stand, by Peter, Ann and William Bateman, 1802. Total weight 19 oz. (all in).

While some of the teapots of the types mentioned bore ornament, the most successful of them were left completely plain except, sometimes, for an engraved crest or coat of arms. A few have been preserved which show a use of the current applied strap-work with accompanying gadrooning, together with spouts moulded and topped with monsters' heads; the latter being a feature especially favoured at the time in France and Germany.

With variations, the bullet teapot remained popular for many years. By 1760 it had begun to acquire a taller pedestal foot, a body shaped like an inverted pear and a curved spout. At the same time, embossing and chasing were freely applied.

After the neo-classical style had gained a hold on design, there came a completely new shape of teapot. During the 1780s an oval vessel with a flat base, a slightly domed cover and a tapering straight spout sprang into favour (see page 50). It was usually accompanied by a stand of the same shape raised on four short feet. Decoration of both items was frequently of neat festoons and bands of leaves in bright cut engraving (Plate 6).

After the turn of the century came a succession of styles including an oblong with rounded corners. Later came revivals of earlier shapes and a liking for the so-called 'melon-shape', which bears in many instances a likeness to a bunch of bananas. About the year 1800, too, came the introduction of matching pieces: jugs, basin and sometimes coffee-pot, all of which were shaped and decorated to match the teapot.

149

The various teapots described are those that would seem to have been the most popular at particular times. Many others had a more limited appeal and survive in quantities suggesting their vogue was only short-lived. Thus, in the decade 1780–90 a number of teapots were made in the popular oval shape, but incorporating a tall-legged stand. Examples of this rather clumsy design, by Andrew Fogelberg and Stephen Gilbert, are modelled with beaded mouldings, festoons of laurels and rams' heads, as well as a bold frieze of scrolling. As Paul Storr served his apprenticeship between about 1785 and 1792 with Fogelberg it is perhaps not surprising that he should have made a teapot of similar pattern in 1799.

Fig. 89
Service, comprising teapot, kettle, milk
jug, water jug, sugar basin and tea caddy.
By John Schofield, 1790. Weight 97 oz.
(all in).

Again, although fashions remained at their peak only for short periods, their appeal never entirely ceased. At the height of rococo elaboration there was always someone who would prefer an unadorned article, or one

150

in what most people would have termed an old-fashioned style. There is also the fact that provincial makers were always some years behind those in the capital.

Fig. 90
Tea service of melon shape with flower knobs on the lids. By Edward, John, William and Edward jr. Barnard, 1831. Weight 73 oz. (all in).

While the bullet teapot had its heyday in London between about 1710 and 1740, a liking for it lingered in the country. One hallmarked 1784, made by J. Hampston and J. Prince of York, is in the Victoria and Albert Museum, and is not the only recorded example of something being made in a manner apparently half-a-century behind the times. This does not, of course, include the very numerous copies of old pieces put on the market in the present century.

TOASTED CHEESE DISHES

For serving toasted cheese a specially-made dish was sometimes provided. In appearance it is similar to an oblong covered entrée dish, with a handle projecting from one of the longer sides. The interior has a false bottom to contain hot water, and above the warmed compartment is a series of small-sized dishes: most of them square, but the corner ones shaped to fit the dish.

The dishes date from the early decades of the nineteenth century, and one amusingly designed example has a lifelike silver mouse climbing up the outside of each corner. The knob handle on the cover is in the shape of a baited mouse-trap.

TOASTING FORKS

The toasting of bread and other eatables was normally carried out in the kitchen with the aid of brass or iron implements. Silver forks were occasionally provided for the purpose, and could be employed by those who preferred to do their own toasting before the dining room or sitting room fire.

Whether he personally used it or not is unknown, but John, Lord Hervey, later first Earl of Bristol possessed one. Evidence of the fact is recorded in his list of expenses, for on 26th July 1711 he noted:

Paid Mr Chambers for mending ye silver toaster, £1.2.s.

In an article in the *Antique Collector* (February 1963) Mr Charles Oman described such forks ranging from an example of 1550, belonging to Henry VIII and melted down 7 years later, to one of late Victorian date. Most of them were made with long turned wood handles, and a number of the metal details were of ingenious design. The accompanying illustrations show eleven specimens ranging in date from 1669 to 1889, all of which are in the Victoria and Albert Museum.

TOAST RACKS

The toast rack, which kept the slices of toasted bread on edge and more or less crisp, has been largely replaced by the electric toaster, which delivers a fresh piece as required. The pre-electricity rack was introduced in about 1770, most examples of the time having detachable wires fitting into an oval base. Towards the end of the century boat-shaped racks were made, and later still the fashion was for oblong ones. They vary in pattern from the completely unadorned to those of Paul Storr, which are typically ornate. One of his, made in 1810, weighs no less than 25 oz., and the wire bars are set in a large oval base decorated with gadroons, reeding and acanthus handles. The central bar is topped by a knob in the form of a bunch of pointed leaves cut short to enclose a rose. This example is 10½ inches long, but the majority are smaller in size and considerably lighter in weight. The average number of bars is seven, which will support six slices of toast.

Fig. 91
Gilt toilet set. By John White, 1727.

TOILET SETS

Silver services for use at the dressing table were made between the Restoration and the mid-eighteenth century. They included a looking glass in a silver frame, candlesticks, small trays, covered boxes and pots, backs for brushes, and such things as snuffers and pincushions. A large one could extend to over thirty separate matching items.

Earlier examples were decorated with embossing and chasing or with cast patterns, and might also be gilt. Others were engraved with Oriental designs. After 1700 they often relied on neat mouldings and the occasional use of gadrooning, with a carefully-engraved coat of arms displayed on each article.

In the second half of the eighteenth century sets were supplied in mahogany boxes, which were given internal divisions to accommodate each article in safety during travel. The boxes, pots and other items were of cut glass with lids of silver invariably bearing the owner's arms, crest or initials.

The services are rarely found now in whatever may have been their complete state. This is usually a matter of conjecture, as the number of items they contained was indefinite and each would have been supplied to a customer's choice. Over the years many of the sets have been dispersed, and the pieces sold individually.

Fig. 92
Pair of tumblers, gilt and matted. Maker's mark R N, 1672. Height 5 inches. Weight 5 oz. 7 dwt.

154

TUMBLERS

Tumblers are short-sided drinking-vessels which have heavy rounded bases, so that when accidentally knocked they right themselves. They were made from the seventeenth century onwards, but were probably not plentiful because written references to them at the time are as few as surviving examples.

Their use was probably confined largely to outdoor occasions, and they formed part of canteens. Two solid gold tumblers of eighteenth century date have been sold by auction in recent years, both of which are engraved with inscriptions recording that they had been awarded to the winners of races held at Chester. This seems to imply a connexion between the vessels and their employment in the open air; the prizes being de-luxe versions of what would have been used at alfresco meals beside the race track.

Fig. 93
Gold tumbler given by Earl Grosvenor as a prize at Chester Races in 1792. By Peter and Ann Bateman, 1791. Height 3½ inches. Weight 9 oz. 11 dwt.

TUREENS

For serving soup at the dining table a tureen, usually oval in shape, was introduced in the early eighteenth century. It was supported on four feet, and both these and the handles at each end of the body and on the lid were the subject of decorative treatment. This varied from decade to decade, but reached its peaks in about 1740–50 and 1810–20. At all periods there were both plain and elaborately ornamented examples from which a buyer might select to suit his taste and pocket. Paul Storr and a few other leading silversmiths of the early 1800s made sets comprising a soup tureen, entrée dishes and sauce tureens, of which the handles to the covers were cast in the form of the owner's crest.

155

Fig. 94
Tureen ornamented with strapwork, shells
and leaves and with a gadrooned rim. By
Henry Herbert, 1738. Width 13 inches.

Fig. 95
Gilt tureen with strapwork ornament and boars' head handles. One of a pair by John Edwards, formerly attributed to John Eckfourd, *circa* 1735. The stands by John Harris, 1818. Width of tureen 15¼ inches. Total weight of tureens with liners and stands 655 oz. 10 dwt.

TWO HANDLED CUPS

The two-handled covered cup was first made in the middle years of the seventeenth century, and the initial type retained its popularity for the ensuing fifty years. Raised on a shallow rim, the body has a rounded base with tall sides varying from straight to curved according to date, and the flanking handles are scrolled. The lid is slightly domed and either has a knob finial or, occasionally, a foot on which it will stand when removed and reversed. Ornamentation is usually by means of embossing and chasing, and while floral compositions predominate, the range includes animals, both real and imaginary, and formal friezes of acanthus leaves. Handles are often topped with female heads, and were either cast or made from curved strips of metal.

Some of the more important covered cups were made with a matching

157

salver on which to stand, but in the majority of surviving examples this appendage, if it existed with them, is now missing. Some of the cups are without covers, and might be referred to more correctly as 'two-handled bowls'. They closely resemble the covered variety, but the upper edge of the body is turned slightly outwards making it appear that they were intended to be open-topped articles.

A rare variety made for a short period after the Restoration has a straight-sided cylindrical body raised on three short feet, and both the cup and its cover have a close-fitting overlay of pierced embossed silver. As the main portion of the vessel is gilt, which shows through the cut-out portions, the contrast is effective against the ungilt casing.

Fig. 96
Two-handled cup and cover, the body embossed and chased with a flower and leaf pattern centred on an elephant bearing on its back a castle, the knob in the form of acanthus leaves. By Richard Stuart, Cork, *circa* 1675. Height 9 inches. Weight 54 oz. 11 dwt.

It was at the turn of the century that the covered cup became imposing; at the time when the refugee French Huguenots were beginning to establish themselves and find a market for articles embodying Continental standards of design and craftsmanship. Under their influence the foot of the cup was made higher, the handles were given greater importance and the body ornamented with all the types of decoration at their command. In addition, from about 1705, a central girdle, which had made an occasional earlier appearance, usually encircles the cup and adds to its distinction. Average examples stand up to twelve inches in height, each has a moulded foot, and the scrolled handles rise to about the level of the rim of the vessel.

Fig. 97
Two-handled cup and cover ornamented with plain and decorated lobes, bold scroll handles and an engraved coat of arms within scroll and leaf mantling. By Pierre Platel, 1707. Height 9¾ inches. Weight 48 oz.

A cup of 1728 by Paul de Lamerie is of this form, but the foot has a band of decoration, while the lower part of the body has applied ornament in the form of upright shaped lobes; plain ones alternating with others cast with a pattern of husks and scrolls. The cover is similarly designed, and the upper part of the body has a band of engraving centred on a coat of arms. Instead of handles of simple curved form, in this instance they are in the van of the rococo and each comprises a large 'C' above a small reversed one.

By 1760 the rococo was fully accepted, and a cup hallmarked the year prior and made by Thomas Heming of Bond Street, London, is typical of the fantasy then current. The cup is of baluster shape raised on a low foot and the cover is domed, with both parts spirally fluted and encrusted all over with a vine and grapes. The upright scrolled handles rise from lion masks and develop into half-figures of Pan, while the whole is topped by a young Bacchus holding aloft a large bunch of grapes. This particular piece is additionally interesting because Heming's trade card, which includes illustrations of half a dozen pieces of silverware, shows at the top left an engraving of a cup of this design.

In a contrasting style to the preceding cup, which is in the Victoria and Albert Museum, is one which was auctioned at Sotheby's in 1969. Hallmarked 1764 it was made by Daniel Smith and Robert Sharp, and is of inverted bell shape raised on a spirally-fluted stem and low foot. The body is chased with garlands and lions' masks, applied with plaques showing horses racing and being exercised and with a frieze depicting horses being ridden. The domed top is decorated with flat leaves and rises to an outward-curving neck with a fluted cover, while the handles are in the shape of winged caryatids.

Fig. 98
Two-handled cup and cover ornamented with neo-classical motifs centred on an oval panel of racing horses and with a finial in the form of a mounted jockey. By William Pitts and Robert Preedy, 1798. Height 21½ inches.

160

Horse-racing was not the only inspiration of designers and makers of cups. Just after the turn of the century a number were made to celebrate the success of Nelson and his men at the Battle of Trafalgar. They were designed by John Flaxman, R.A., and presented by Lloyd's Patriotic Fund to the admirals and captains who had fought in the battle, which took place on 21st October, 1805.

The Trafalgar Vases stand 17 inches in height, with a figure of Britannia on one side of the bell-shaped body and Hercules and the Hydra on the other. On the top stands a realistic figure of a lion, and other ornament takes the form of scrolling foliage and rosettes, acanthus leaves and groups of acorns. The handles rise straight from the sides and curl inwards level with the finial.

At all periods many of the cups and covers were gilt. This not only had the effect of greatly enhancing their appearance, but meant that they needed less frequent cleaning. Thus, most of those that were so treated are in considerably better condition than the plain silver examples.

WAX JACKS

As an alternative to the taper box, a length of taper for letter-sealing could be kept handy in a wax jack. It is a small-sized open stand enclosing a reel turned by means of a cranked handle. The taper is unwound from the reel and led up through an orifice, which is usually a spring-loaded scissor-pattern device. An alternative pattern dispenses with the reel and handle, and the taper is coiled round an upright post.

Surviving examples of wax jacks date from the mid-eighteenth century onwards, but it is likely that they were in use earlier and that they were employed prior to the introduction of the taper box.

See **TAPER BOXES**

WINE CISTERNS

In order to cool wine prior to serving it at a large gathering, bottles and jugs of it were placed in a cistern filled with cold water. It is known that Queen Elizabeth I owned a cistern made of silver which weighed 525 oz. 10 dwt., but like many others of later date it no longer exists. Quite a number remain, however, that were made subsequent to the Restoration.

The most famous of all is larger than any other, measuring 5 ft. 6 in. across the handles and weighing 7,221 oz. It was the work of Charles Kandler in 1734, to the order of Henry Jerningham, who was described at the time as being a banker, a jeweller or a goldsmith, and was possibly a combination of all three. A year after he acquired it the owner obtained the necessary Parliamentary permission to hold a lottery, and tickets were offered to the public. The winner was a Sussex landowner, Major William Battine, and within a year or two he had disposed of his prize to the Empress Anne of Russia, niece of Peter the Great.

The cistern is still in Russia, although no longer in Royal ownership, but copies of it can be seen in the Victoria and Albert Museum, London, and the Metropolitan Museum, New York. It has been pointed out that it is likely to be more helpful to inspect the original or the copies than to read a description. True enough, but it may be mentioned that the vast oval basin rests on four panthers or leopards, while the rim is almost hidden under branches of vine leaves and clusters of grapes.

Fig. 99
Wine cistern formerly in the possession of the Dukes of Sutherland and now in the Minneapolis Institute of Art. By Paul de Lamerie, 1719. Width 38 inches. Weight 700 oz. 5dwt.

Dr N. M. Penzer recorded twenty-seven cisterns, including the one above, which were made in the eighteenth century and are still in existence (see *Apollo*, September 1957). One other, made in the nineteenth

162

century, is as notable in its way as the Kandler example. It was made by John Bridge in 1828/9 to the order of George IV, although as the King died in 1830 it is doubtful that he ever saw it in its finished state. The cistern is of silver-gilt, measures 4 ft. 6 in. in width and weighs about 8,000 oz. The body represents a series of half-open clam shells revealing bacchanals, and the handles are in the form of the supporters of the Royal arms, the lion and the unicorn. The stem and base of the pedestal are modelled with seaweed, coral and other forms of marine life, and the four feet conceal a set of castors.

There are two amusing contemporary records of this mighty vessel in use at Windsor Castle. In one, it was related that on the occasion of the birthday of William IV, on the 31st August 1830, John Bridge was allowed the privilege of being present, 'and was hid during the dinner behind the great wine cooler'. In the other, the cistern was described as being used in 1842 at the christening of the Prince of Wales, later Edward VII. It was filled for the occasion not with Jordan water, as might be expected, but with mulled claret!

WINE FUNNELS

The earliest recorded wine funnel dates back to 1651, but until the advent of the glass decanter they were not made in any quantity. After the mid-eighteenth century there was a big output of them to cater for the increasing number of people who laid down port and decanted it for use. The funnels are of plain pattern, strictly functional in appearance, but relieved by a gadrooned or beaded rim and perhaps a band or two of simple moulding. The interior has a strainer which can be removed for cleaning, and the narrow end of the tapering tube is usually divided by a V-shaped cut.

The funnel is completed by a saucer-like dish with a central dome on which it rests, inverted, when not in use.

WINE AND SAUCE LABELS

In about 1755 there was introduced a glass decanter on which was engraved the name of the wine it should contain. The first mention of these vessels appeared in the *Norwich Mercury* for 26th December 1755, which announced

. . . new-fashioned decanters with inscriptions engraven on them, Port, Claret, Mountain, etc., etc., decorated with vine leaves, grapes, etc.

In due course decanters in blue, green and amethyst glass with the names of their proposed contents written in gold lettering began to be

163

made. They were all suggested by a new device that had recently been put on the market by silversmiths: known then as a bottle ticket, but nowadays called a wine label.

The forerunner of the silver label had been a scrap of paper or parchment recording the contents of a bottle, but with more refined manners came other improvements. The dark glass bottle no longer came to polite tables, and its place was taken by the decanter. The latter bore round its neck a small label on a chain, or announced what it held by engraved lettering on the glass surface.

Considerable study has been given to the labels, and there are collections to be seen in London at the Victoria and Albert Museum and the London Museum, and the New York Historical Society possesses a large quantity. In spite of the feverish interest in them they are still obtainable, although at prices very much enhanced from those of only a few years ago.

The labels were made in many patterns ranging from simple lettered oblongs to elaborate shapes embossed, chased and gilded. The various designs were classified by Dr N. M. Penzer as follows:

1 Narrow rectangular.

2 Escutcheon or shield.

3 Crescent.

4 Vine and tendril.

5 Goblet and festoons.

6 Scroll.

7 Festooned drapery.

8 Broad rectangular.

9 Shell.

10 Cupids, grapes and satyrs.

11 Single vine leaf.

12 Oval.

13 Kidney shape.

14 Armorial.

15 Cut-out capital letter.

16 Cut-out word.

17 Architectural.

18 Neck-rings.

19 Curios.

20 Miscellaneous.

Fig. 100
Wine labels: (top row) CLARET, by
C. Reily and G. Storer, *circa* 1830;
SHERRY, by Thomas Phipps and
Edward Robinson, 1806; (centre row)
WHITE WINE, by Hester Bateman,

circa 1775; PORT, by Benjamin and
James Smith, *circa* 1810; MOUNTAIN
DEW, by Sandylands Drinkwater, *circa*
1750; (bottom row) MADEIRA, by
Paul Storr, 1815; WHISKEY, by C. T.
and G. Fox, 1845.

165

It should be explained that 'Curios' (19) includes labels made from boars' tusks and tigers' claws mounted in silver and needless to say, the last category, 'Miscellaneous' is the biggest of all. Silversmiths and their patrons gave full rein to their fancy in making labels, and some most unusual designs have been recorded.

Many of the eighteenth century wine labels bear only the stamp of the maker. In fact, they were exempted from assay until 1790, but in spite of that silversmiths sometimes submitted them voluntarily and the labels bear a full set of marks. After 1790 they should have been sent to Goldsmiths' Hall in the normal way, but not all makers were punctilious in doing so. It involved the payment of duty, and although the amount was trifling it was all too often dodged.

While the many shapes taken by labels are intriguing a similar appeal lies in the numerous names they bear. Some are of well-known beverages, others are of long-forgotten ones, while quite a few are the result of misspellings on somebody's part. These last can cause many hours to be wasted in fruitless research, but others reveal interesting facets of social history that might otherwise be missed.

For instance, Gin is found engraved clearly on many labels, but is also known rendered as Nig, Cream of the Valley and Old Tom, perhaps in attempts to hoodwink thirsty servants or to defeat the prying eyes of visitors. Wines such as Bucellas, Mountain, Bronte and Calcavella were once very popular, as is attested by the numerous labels bearing their names. Mysteries include inscriptions reading Paid, Pando, Calamity Water and quite a few others figured among the 1,500 or so names which have been listed.

Sauces and lotions were labelled in a manner similar to wines, although chiefly during the nineteenth century. Sauce labels are usually smaller in size than others, as they were hung round the necks of bottles held in cruets. A set of thirteen, hallmarked 1807 and now belonging to the New York Historical Society, is typical of most of the type. They bear the following names, which pose some tricky problems of identification:

Quin's Sauce.	Cavice.
Soy.	Coratch.
Anchovy.	Zoobditty-Match.
Tomato.	Piquante.
Ketchup.	Royal.
Chili Vinegar.	Camp.
Harvey.	

166

Lotions and perfume labels include such preparations as Bergamot, Frangipanni, Milk of Roses, Eau de Pluie (pure rain-water, for the complexion) and Tooth Mixture.

A considerable number of silversmiths are recorded as having made labels during the eighteenth and nineteenth centuries. They include many men who are comparatively unknown, but also others like Paul Storr, members of the Bateman family and Sandylands Drinkwater who, in spite of his surname, is thought to have made some of the very first wine labels.

The history of wine labels was first recorded painstakingly by the late Dr N. M. Penzer in his *Book of the Wine Label*, published in 1947. More recently, the subject has been brought up to date by the Reverend E. W. Whitworth (*Wine Labels*, in Cassell's *Collectors' Pieces* series, 1966), who is Honorary Secretary of the Wine Label Circle. The members of the latter make a study of labels, discuss them at meetings and publish a Journal.

Glossary of Terms

Acanthus: A plant common in the Mediterranean area, which has deeply cut, large and shiny leaves. It was adopted by the Greeks as a decorative motif and its use in this role spread westwards as the centuries advanced.

Anthemion: Another motif owed to the ancient Greeks, and although it closely resembles the flower of the well-known honeysuckle it was originally taken from that of the acanthus.

Baluster: A pear-shaped form, 'slender above and bulging below', which owes its name to its connexion with the balustrade or baluster; the latter now corrupted to 'banister'.

Bead: Half-sphere used to form decorative borders.

Bell-shape: Resembling a bell: curved at the shoulders and splaying at the base.

Caryatid: A human figure, usually female, forming the upper part of a column.

Cut-card: A type of ornament made by cutting a sheet of silver to a desired shape and then soldering it to the main article. It served as decoration, and at the same time was a useful way of adding strength.

Fluting: Channels chased or cast on the surface of a piece.

Flying-scroll: A handle so-described is fixed to the body of an article only by its lower end.

Gadrooning: A row of lobes usually set at an angle to right or left.

Guilloche: A band of decoration composed of two or more interwoven ribbons with flowers or paterae in the spaces.

Husks: A garland formed of wheat husks. It was once said they represented the catkins of the shrub *Garrya Elliptica*, but it has been pointed out that this was not introduced into Europe from California until the nineteenth century.

Matted Ground: Either a roughened background to contrast with polished embossing and chasing, or a gilt surface left dull against burnished portions.

Paterae: Circular or oval ornaments of classical design.

Reeding: Raised ribs, the opposite of fluting, used alone or as border patterns. In the latter instance they are found 'tied' at intervals with ribbons, and the pattern is known as reed-and-tie or reed-and-ribbon.

Strapwork: Lengths of straight or curved flat ribbon or strapping employed as decoration.

Thread Edge: A term used to describe two or more lines of narrow reeding, resembling threads, used often round the edge of spoon and fork handles.

APPENDIX

BOOKS ON OLD SILVER CURRENTLY AVAILABLE

Title	Author	Publisher	Price
Collecting English Silver	M. Curran	Arco Publ.	25s. 0d.
English Silver	J. Stone	Cory, Adams & Mackay	30s. 0d.
English Silver	J. Banister	Ward, Lock & Co.	35s. 0d.
English Domestic Silver	C. Oman	Adam & Charles Black	30s. 0d.
Silver Collecting for Amateurs	J. Henderson	Frederick Muller	18s. 0d.
Adam Silver	R. Rowe	Faber & Faber	63s. 0d.
Old Table Silver	H. Brunner	Faber & Faber	84s. 0d.
Victorian Silver	P. Wardle	Herbert Jenkins	50s. 0d.
An Introduction to Old English Silver	J. Banister	Evans Brothers	50s. 0d.
English and other Silver	Y. Hackenbrock	Thames & Hudson	189s. 0d.
Silver Boxes	E. Delieb	Herbert Jenkins	70s. 0d.
English Silver Drinking Vessels to 1830	D. Ash	G. Bell & Son Ltd.	30s. 0d.
Silver	C. Dunning & P. E. Plow	Golden West, U.S.A.	$5.95
Silver	R. Came	Putnam, U.S.A.	$5.95
American Silver Manufacturers	D. T. Rainwater	Nelson, U.S.A.	$10.00
Silver	G. Taylor	Penguin, U.S.A.	$2.45

Index